Bridge of the turbine express steamer "Imperator".
Below: longitudinal section of the "Imperator".

Otto J. Seiler

BRIDGE ACROSS THE ATLANTIC

The Story of Hapag-Lloyd's
North American Liner Services

SEIT  1789

Verlag E. S. Mittler & Sohn GmbH
Herford

Foreword

On 6 October 1683, thirteen families from Krefeld set foot on American soil at Philadelphia, thereby marking the beginning of German settlement in America.

In the course of the past three centuries more than seven million Germans followed them. Today there are over fifty million Americans of German descent.

For most emigrants who made their way to America from Germany and Eastern Europe, Bremen and Hamburg were the last German cities they saw on their journey to their new homeland. And it was on ships from Hamburg and Bremen that they crossed the Atlantic.

I appreciate it that this year, in which the tricentennial of German settlement in America is being commemorated on both sides of the Atlantic, Hapag-Lloyd is drawing attention to an anniversary that is important not only for its own history.

135 years ago Hamburg-Amerikanische Packetfahrt-Actien-Gesellschaft inaugurated the first regular ocean liner service between Hamburg and New York with its three-masted clipper "Deutschland". Norddeutscher Lloyd of Bremen soon followed suit.

With ever bigger and faster ships these two companies built a bridge across the Atlantic.

The 135-year history of their North America services is a true reflection of the success of German shipping and the reverses of fortune sustained during those eventful times.

I trust that this documentation will find many interested readers.

Karl Carstens

Der Bundespräsident   Bonn, im November 1983

                    G e l e i t w o r t

Mit 13 Familien aus Krefeld, die am 6. Oktober 1683
in Philadelphia amerikanischen Boden betraten,
begann die deutsche Einwanderung in Amerika.

Ihnen folgten im Laufe der vergangenen drei Jahrhun-
derte über sieben Millionen Deutsche. Heute gibt es
mehr als 50 Millionen Amerikaner deutscher Abstam-
mung.

·Für die Mehrzahl der Auswanderer, die aus Deutschland
und Osteuropa den Weg nach Amerika suchten, waren
Bremen und Hamburg die letzten deutschen Städte,
die sie auf ihrer Reise in die neue Heimat sahen,
auf Schiffen aus Hamburg und Bremen überquerten sie
den Atlantik.

Ich begrüße es, daß die Hapag-Lloyd AG in diesem Jahr,
in dem auf beiden Seiten des Atlantik an die 300. Wieder-
kehr der ersten deutschen Auswanderung nach Amerika
erinnert wird, auf ein nicht nur für ihre Firmenge-
schichte wichtiges Jubiläum hinweist: Vor 135 Jahren
nahm die Hamburg-Amerikanische Packetfahrt-Actien-
Gesellschaft mit dem Dreimaster "Deutschland" den
ersten regelmäßigen Schiffsverkehr zwischen Hamburg
und New York auf. Der Bremer Norddeutsche Lloyd folgte
bald darauf.

Mit immer größeren und schnelleren Schiffen haben
diese beiden Gesellschaften eine Brücke über den
Atlantik geschlagen.

Die 135jährige Geschichte der Nordamerika-Dienste
ist ein getreuer Spiegel der Erfolge deutscher
Schiffahrt wie der Schicksalsschläge, die sie in
wechselvollen Zeitläufen erleiden mußte.

Ich wünsche dem Buch aufgeschlossene Leser.

                    Karl Carstens

Contents

Introduction

More than 50 Million Americans living in the USA today have German ancestors, who, at one point in the past decided to leave their homeland in order to start a new and better life in America. Against the background of the Tricentennial of the beginning of German emigration to North America Hapag-Lloyd AG thought that it might be worth recording how and under what conditions the greater part of the 7 million Germans as well as other European emigrants travelled to their new home.

As sucessor company of the two big shipping companies that carried the majority of German and a considerable number of other European emigrants to the US following the inauguration of their competitive liner services in 1848 and 1858 the double jubilee appeared to be a worthy occasion, in a critical review and prospect, to give an account of how successfully the two founding companies, Hapag and Lloyd, have been in establishing a permanent bridge across the Atlantic. Not only has this bridge fostered German-American relations to the benefit of their mutual foreign trade, it has also strengthened their countries' cultural ties.

Hapag and Lloyd would probably have disappeared long ago had it not been for the confidence and consistent support of a significant number of European and American passengers and shippers over the decades, particularly after the long interruptions forced upon them by the two World Wars. This confidence encouraged and enabled the two companies to rebuild and continue to serve their customers on both sides of the Ocean.

Therefore, this book is dedicated to the great number of American and European friends of Hapag-Lloyd AG in commemoration of these Tricentennial celebrations, which also marked the 135th year of Hapag-Lloyd's services to the United States: On October 15th, 1848, the 3-masted Clipper "Deutschland" inaugurated a regular Transatlantic mail, passenger and liner cargo service from Hamburg to New York with 16 cabin and 74 steerage passengers on board.

Until today, this trade route connecting the Old and the New World has always remained the cornerstone of Hapag-Lloyd's worldwide shipping activities. Ever since it has constituted the "highway of world seaborne trade", which in many respects decisively influenced the direction of ocean shipping. New vessel types and technological developments were tested on the North Atlantic route first, with the objective, if possible, of always being ahead of competitors by at least "a ship's length".

For more than a century Hapag-Lloyd and their founding companies belong to the leading carriers in this Trade.

The private publication of 1983 has long been out of print and is now presented in a second revised and updated version and in an even more beautiful layout by E. S. Mittler & Sohn GmbH, Herford.

Full-rigged clipper "Oder"
of 690 grt commissioned
by Hapag in 1851 for the
Hamburg—New York
route; painting from
Roger Chapelet, collection
Hapag-Lloyd AG.

Keen competition between the two old hanseatic cities, Bremen and Hamburg, as trading partners of the USA (1783–1983)

When the Hamburg-America Line (also known as HAPAG) and North German Lloyd (or Lloyd) were founded in 1847 and 1857 respectively, as the leading shipping companies of their home ports Hamburg and Bremen, Germany was still divided into 35 small sovereign kingdoms, duchies and free cities, all loosely connected under the Confederation of German States, whose Parliament resided at Frankfurt. From the mediaeval days of the famous "League of the Hanse" up to the present, Hamburg and Bremen have maintained a certain political independence as city-states. Each has a democratic constitution similar to that of the US, with a Governing Mayor as well as a Senate and a House of Representatives, the latter being elected by the democratic vote of their citizens.

Prior to the unification of Germany by the Prussian Prime Minister Otto von Bismarck in 1868–71, these Hanseatic Cities, with their own independent missions abroad, had been among the first to recognize the US as an independent country. The US policy of maintaining open ports to all nations put an end to the trade monopolies of the old colonial powers. For the first time, German shipping companies were given the chance to participate in overseas trading. Bremen and Hamburg were quick to make full use of this new "freedom of the oceans". Already by 1795, they were the scond most important export partners of the US after Great Britain. Between 1790 and 1799 their imports from the US rose from US$ 425,000 to US$ 17,250,000.

The Napoleonic Wars, however, interrupted these commercial links for almost a decade and inflicted serious damage on these Hanseatic cities' overseas trading and shipping activities, and the number of ships dropped to an all time low. In the years needed for recovery, US flag carriers filled the gap. In the period from 1815 to 1830, US flag ships outnumbered German vessels sailing to North America from Hamburg and Bremen. In the first half of the 19th century, US shipyards produced some of the finest wooden clippers in the world, whose excellent sailing qualities and solid construction were of high repute.

It was also during this time that Bremen became the leading German port for North American trade. Thanks to the foresight of its mayor, Johann Smidt, a new deepsea port called Bremerhaven was built at the Weser estuary in 1830. While Hamburg was dedicating its main activities to trades with the newly established independent Latin American states, Bremen became the most important European port for American tobacco and cotton. More significantly, Bremen also took an early interest in attracting German emigrants to the Weser port for embarkation to the New World.

In 1840, the Cunard Line with the aid of British Government subsidies, established the first regular Transatlantic steam packet service from Liverpool to Boston via Halifax with wooden paddle steamers. American business circles considered it desirable to break this British monopoly and were determined to initiate a competitive American flag service from New York to a suitable European port. As soon as this news reached Bremen, its Senate took great pains in competing with other ports to be chosen as the European terminal. Bremen eventually did succeed in becoming the new center for the American mail service.

To fulfil the five-year mail contract awarded by the US Postmaster General for a fortnightly service between New York and Bremen, the OCEAN STEAM NAVIGATION COMPANY was founded in May of 1846. A third of the shares were placed with US business circles, while Bremen was able to persuade several German state governments, including Prussia, Hanover, Oldenburg, Saxony, Baden and the city of Frankfurt to acquire shares. It was for the first time since centuries that overriding maritime interests induced several German Federal states to a concerted action.

In March 1847 as a preliminary of the new service a postal agreement was concluded between the American Postmaster General and the city of Bremen in which the municipal post office at Bremen became the exclusive agency for the US mails to Germany and the adjacent countries under determination of the postal fees that had to be charged. Since the postal fees were only half of those for transshipment via the United Kingdom, within a couple of weeks all German postal authorities acceded to the agreement, with the result, that the German postal unity in the traffic with the USA came about already 24 years prior to the foundation of the German empire.

This first four-weekly postal steamer service to Germany had, however, to be terminated after only ten years: for when the annual subsidy of 100,000 dollars per ship of the postal contract was up for renewal for a further five years in 1857, the US Senate decided to offer this contract to the lowest bidder, irrespective of the already existing service, which in this case happened to be Commodore Vanderbilt. Taking into account that only a year earlier Hapag had started a service of iron screw-steamers from Hamburg to New York and that a screw-steamship service was also about to be launched by Norddeutscher Lloyd (North German Lloyd) in Bremen, the Ocean Line board of directors considered their wooden paddle steamers too old to compete successfully with these modern services and, after losing the financial backing of the US mail contract, the Ocean Line suspended operations in July of 1857. By the time the two ships were offered for sale, the US was facing one of its severest economic depressions and consequently, the company was liquidated with the loss of two-thirds of its capital.

Hamburg-America Line (HAPAG): It all started with sailing ships (1848)

On May 27, 1847, one year after the Ocean Line, the HAMBURG-AMERIKANISCHE PACKETFAHRT-ACTIEN-GESELLSCHAFT (HAPAG) was founded, being registered in Hamburg with a capital of 300,000 Mark banco.

Known in Germany as "Hapag", in Hamburg as „Packetfahrt", it became the "Hamburg-America Line" in English.

In the statutes that were issued by the constituent general meeting the following was stated about the aims of the company:

"Hapag's objective is the establishment of a regular connection between Hamburg and North America by means of sailing ships under the Hamburg flag and for that purpose, as far as the capital allows, the necessary ships will be built and purchased, in case of need also chartered. The ships are in the first instance intended for the route from and to New York."

The founding fathers — comprising 41 shareholders altogether — included such prominent Hamburg merchants and shipowners as the ship broker August Bolten, who in 1871 also founded Hamburg's second largest shipping company, the Hamburg-South America Line, better known these days in the United States as Columbus Line; Ferdinand Laeisz, the founder of the shipping company F. Laeisz, whose famous four-masted barques — so-called flying P-Liners — rounded Cape Horn in record time; and Adolph Godeffroy, Hapag's first Chairman of the Board. Godeffroy directed the company's fortunes with great skill for the first 33 years.

In 1847, steamships were still in their infancy. It was thus a sober and wise decision by Hapag's founding management not to start with steamships, given the modest financial resources at its disposal and the lack of financial backing from any powerful national government.

In spite of the scarce funds, great importance was attached to the acquisition of efficient, solid and fast sailing vessels when contracting the new buildings. For that purpose several ship yards on the German coasts, as well as in Finland, Sweden and Denmark were invited to tender. The first three sailing ships were ordered from Hamburg yards. The fourth vessel could be acquired on the slip-way at Bremerhaven for an exceptionally favourable price.

The German-Danish war that had meanwhile broken out, delayed delivery of the three Hamburg ships by several months. In spite of receiving additional payments, both ship yards suffered severe losses, as they had not built such large ships before and had, therefore, miscalculated the costs.

In October 15, 1848 the clipper "Deutschland" of 500 grt and 700 tons carrying capacity inaugurated the new regular North Atlantic service under the Hamburg flag — a German flag still did not exist at that time. The other three vessels were of similar size with accommodation for 20 cabin and 200 steerage passengers and entered the service during the winter months 1848/49 under the names "Nord-Amerika", "Rhein" and "Elbe". They were manned by a crew of between 15 and 17 seamen and had a limited cargo capacity.

August Bolten, as Hapag's permanent port agent, was able to offer facilities which, at that time, were the exception rather than the rule in ocean transport.

Adolph Godeffroy made the following remarkable statement during the general meeting in December 1848 about the accommodation and operation of the first Hapag vessels:

"All three vessels have turned out very beautifully. The cabin and steerage accommodation are, without any undue luxury, as pretty and comfortable as one could have wished. Each ship has a small library on board. All crockery has the name of the ship engraved, and there is a plentiful supply of linen for the needs of the passengers. Care was taken in particular to provide a bed for each passenger."

"The benefit of this comfortable accommodation has already proved its value, for passengers, who had the intention to travel with ships of other shipping companies, upon inspection of our ships, chose the latter."

„Care was taken in particular to entrust the command of the ships to efficient captains, who are not only efficient seamen, but also people, who by their friendly, courteous, and sociable

The main mast of the "Deutschland" passed through the middle of the gentlemen's salon.

The ladie's lounge was in the ship's stern.

The 3-mast-clippers "Deutschland" (717 dwt) and "Nordamerika" (558 dwt) inaugurated Hamburg-America Line's regular mail, cargo and passenger service to North America in 1848.

The new 2,250 ton iron screw-steamer "Bremen", built by Caird & Co., Greenock, inaugurated North German Lloyd's Trans-Atlantic Service from Bremerhaven to New York in June, 1858.
(Focke-Museum, Bremen)

The express-steamer
"Deutschland" of 16,500 grt,
was Hapag's only four-funnel
ship. On her maiden voyage
in July, 1900 she won the
"Blue Ribbon" with an
average of 23,36 knots and
she was able to maintain
this title for the following
two years.

Before 1914 the 25,570 grt "George Washington" was North German Lloyd's Flag ship. The above painting shows her arrival at the port of New York. The ship's staircase and lounges of the First class were decorated with paintings by the German artist Prof. Bruno Paul showing the places of activity of the first US President.

Page 12

The "Kronprinzessin Cecilie", 19,500 grt, 23 knots, named after the German emperor's eldest daughter, was the last ship of the famous express steamer quartet, which North German Lloyd commissioned between 1897 and 1907, and was a very popular ship among American passengers. With these four ships NGL could offer a weekly express service. The other ships of that class were "Kaiser Wilhelm der Große" (1897), Blue Ribbon winner from 1897 until 1900, "Kronprinz Wilhelm" (1901) and "Kaiser Wilhelm II" (1903), holder of the Blue Ribbon from 1904 until 1906.

12

character will render life on board as comfortable as possible for the passengers, and one has been fortunate in this regard to have made a very good selection."

"The captains and mates have been given a uniform of their own, and in consideration of their rank on board, a comprehensive instruction has been issued for them. Since a similar pakket service does not yet exist here, it had been the aim of the directors to create something extraordinary, and for that reason the whole undertaking was planned from the outset, being internally solid and respectable through and through, whilst outwardly also providing it with the necessary glamour. The directors have been guided in doing so by the standard of the steam packet of the Austrian Lloyd."

"The directors have also introduced so-called conduite-books, one for the cabin and one for the steerage, which the captain is obliged to present to the passengers each time after completion of a voyage, so that they may record their views about the treatment on board. This arrangement has found already imitation in Bremen..."

New standards were also created with regard to reliability of the service. The average length of a Hapag packet voyage was about 40 days westbound and 28 days eastbound. In contrast, 70 to 100 days were by no means unusual for other shipping lines.

In the A.G.M. the following was reported about the maiden voyage of the "Nord-Amerika":

"The second ship that entered the trade, "Nord-Amerika", arrived in New York after a quick voyage. Although the captain had the misfortune that the breakage of the main yard caused the death of the first mate and the injury of seven of the crew, with the result that for a time the captain had to manoeuvre the ship with the remaining 8 crew members, the vessel from Portsmouth has still beaten almost all packets that had left Le Havre and Liverpool simultaneously and performed an extremely quick voyage in 35 days."

The first full business year of 1849 was overshadowed by the German-Danish war. Due to the blockade of the Elbe by a Danish fleet, the ships, with the exception of the "Deutschland", could each only accomplish one instead of three round voyages. The "Deutschland" succeeded in breaking the blockade under Russian flag. A Swedish charter vessel fully booked with emigrants could also pass the blockade uninhibited from Cuxhaven. Due to the rapid rise of the number of emigrants, 13 ships had to be chartered additionally in 1851 and a fifth larger sailing ship, the "Oder" was purchased. She had space for 40 cabin and 250 steerage passengers.

Hapag's ships and staff soon acquired a high reputation, and by the spring of 1850 a network of agencies had been well established throughout Germany.

After the fifth year of business, shareholders received their first dividend, and for the ensuing decade the Hapag sailing packets proved a complete success. By 1858 a total of 8 sailing packets were trading under the Hapag flag.

The first steamships (1856)

Although Hapag's sailing packets performed faster voyages than the Cunard steamship "British Queen" – "Rhein" made the quickest westbound voyage in 26 days and "Donau" the quickest homeward voyage in 19 days – the advantages of steam navigation not only for passenger shipping but also for cargo traffic became ever more evident. Already a significant passenger traffic began from the USA to Europe, which the steam packets completely absorbed.

Taking this development into full account in good time, Godeffroy called an extraordinary general meeting in January 1854, in which it was unanimously decided to acquire two big screw steamships to enhance the sailing fleet which in the meantime had increased to 6 vessels.

His impressive trend-setting reasoning is captivating still today, one hundred and thirty-seven years later:

"The possible further increase of our sailing packets, by clippers in particular, must be reserved for later approval. Today we must address ourselves to more urgent matters, namely the acquisition of big screw steamships, the employment of which in our service has now become a necessity, if we do not wish to be overtaken by our active neighbouring city Bremen, by our dangerous competitor Antwerp, where steam packets either already exist or have already been commenced upon in a magnificant manner; and if we do not want to readily leave the territory gained by the effiency of our ships and the steady advance with the requirements of the time, to the more active and prudent competitors; if we wish not to permit Hamburg's prospering traffic with North America to slacken and to allow it to fall back into second class. Furthermore, the paramount competition of England, although more distant, must not be overlooked, where currently steam shipping is expanding in a gigantic way."

"Too long already Hamburg has remained behind such a development of commercial enterprise, and in this respect our company seems to us to be primarily called upon to take the initiative on behalf of Germany's leading trading city."

That is the proper spirit, which one generation later promoted Albert Ballin and Heinrich Wiegand, to lead Hapag and Lloyd to the top of the large shipping companies of the world. Until then much rough ground and many turbulent storms had still to be overcome.

The capital required for the first two steamers was three times as high as the sum total of the company's sailing fleet investments so far. The capital had, therefore, to be increased by two million marks banco by dissolving the company's reserve funds and by issuing bearer stocks. The founding capital had been raised through the issuance of registered stocks restricted to Hamburg citizens.

Since at that time German ship yards were still not capable of building ocean steamships of that size, orders were placed with Caird & Co of Greenock in Scotland for two iron steamships of 2,000 grt, 1000 tons carrying capacity and a service speed of 12 knots. They were christened "Borussia" and "Hammonia", the Latin names of Prussia and Hamburg, which were easier for foreigners to pronounce. This Hapag tradition of giving its ships the latinised names of German towns, provinces and federal states continued until only recently, when it was ordering the seven racy multipurpose cargo liners of the "Westfalia"-class of 12,544 tdw and 21 knots between 1964/1966 for employment in the Far East, from Blohm & Voss, the Hamburg ship yard.

Germany was then also still lacking ship engineers. Hapag's revised company statutes directed, however, that all ships be manned by German crews. For that purpose, the German engineer Jacob Diederichsen, who

13

had served in the Prussian Navy and was reputed to be an extraordinarily efficient man, was entrusted with the ship building supervision in Greenock and became the chief engineer of Hapag's first steamship.

The ratings were also trained for the special requirements of the steamship service and proper operational regulations had been devised. Until completion of their ships, the captains had to serve on foreign flag steamers, in order to familiarise themselves with the command of such ships.

Again political events overshadowed the company's affairs. A strike at Greenock delayed delivery of the vessels until the late summer of 1854 and prompted the directors to charter out the two vessels at favourable conditions to the British and French governments for repatriation of troops from the Crimean War. This provided an ideal opportunity for the commands and crew to gain much needed experience with the new ships.

Eventually, on June 1st, 1856 the "Borussia" left Hamburg after a one year delay as the first ship on its inaugural trip to New York, where she arrived on schedule on June 15th. The "Hammonia" followed four weeks later. As of December 1857 the service was extended by including intermediate calls at Southampton on both the outward and homeward voyages.

As far as speed, fixtures and furnishings were concerned, the vessels fully met the design specifications. Only the prescribed draft of 17 feet was substantially exceeded, with the result that the steamers hat to be loaded and discharged in the Hamburg roads, which necessitated the acquisition of a lighter fleet.

In their external appearance the first steamships still looked like sailing ships but with a funnel. The Hapag chronicler Kurt Himer characterises them as genuine three-masted barques, the full rigging of which had to guarantee that, in the event of a serious engine defect or of a not uncommon breakage of the crankshaft, the voyage could be continued.

The inauguration of this regular four-weekly steamship connection stimulated the passenger and goods traffic to the United States to such an extent, that two further larger steamships, the "Austria" and "Saxonia" were ordered in the same year, in order to upgrade the service to fortnightly sailings. Again orders were placed at favourable conditions at Greenock.

Unfortunately, the "Austria" was haunted by bad luck. Initial problems with the machinery twice in succession on her outbound voyage caused the British government to cancel a charter for the carriage of troops to suppress the Sepoy Mutiny in India. Later, the ship caught fire on her third outward North Atlantic voyage when a boatswain lost control of a red-hot chain, used to fumigate emigrant quarters with tar, thereby setting the wooden deck aflame. Fanned by a strong wind, the ship was ablaze from stem to stern within a few minutes. The result was 471 casualties out of the 538 passengers and crew — unquestionably one of the most tragic events in the history of this company.

The material loss was replaced by the acquisition of two steamships of equal size, the "Bavaria" and "Teutonia", from the fleet of a bankrupt shipping company.

In the annual report the following was stated about this transaction: "The acquisition of the "Teutonia" seemed to us just as important, since without a reserve ship in case of an accident, albeit of an insignificant nature, an interruption of the service was inevitable. We have had sufficient opportunity to fully convince ourselves that it is ostensibly the assured regularity of our vessels' dispatch, which is the best guarantee for the profitability of the company."

Right from the start planning and organization of the new steamship line was directed towards a high standard of service and reliability. As at that time Hamburg had no quays to receive these large vessels, Hapag purchased barges, tenders and floating cranes to expedite the turnround of the ships. In 1858 extensive quay facilities in the central port area with warehouses and direct train connections with Kiel, Berlin and Hamburg, were acquired, thereby saving passengers and cargo the inconvenience of having to be transferred by rivercraft to and from the ocean ships. At Steinwerder, on the other side of the river at the port of Hamburg, a ship's supply magazine was established, which proved to be the predecessor of Hapag's extensive technical works in later years, which still exist today, although on a more modest scale. Similar facilities were acquired from the city of New York at Hoboken.

In order to avoid sending the steamships to British shipyards each time their hulls needed cleaning or repair work to sea damage had to be performed, the directors repeatedly urged the supervisory board to have a drydock built in Hamburg, to which they finally agreed in 1865. After several constructional mishaps, it was ultimately completed in March 1870 and proved to be a full success for several decades.

The first three full business years of the steamship service of 1857/59 were to be overshadowed by severe international economic depression and war, which could not be counterbalanced by whatever careful planning and organisation of Hapag's management. In the Annual Report of 1859 it was stated:

"The results of the year 1859 are, unfortunately, not of the kind that would enable the payment of a dividend. As in 1857 the severe trade depression and in 1858 its deeply negative consequences had a disastrous effect on trade and shipping and thus also paralysed the development of our company. During the last year the initial uncertainty of the general political conditions and later the actual outbreak of war destroyed our legitimate hopes."

The same report recorded at another place, however, and not without pride:

"The steamships of our company have during the past year performed their service with exceptional punctuality — a dispatch day was never neglected — and the confidence of the public on this side as well as on the other side of the ocean is definitely turning more and more to our line."

Due to the continuing outward cargo traffic, the North Atlantic service was for the first time also maintained during the winter months of 1859. In previous years the ships had to be laid up between November and March due to lack of employment.

In 1866 a weekly service could be offered to and from New York with a fleet of 6 steamers.

On Oct. 1st, 1867, the 2,250 ton "Bavaria" started a new service from Hamburg via Havana to New Orleans with monthly sailings.

In December of 1871, the city of Hamburg commissioned its first icebreaker, substantially financed by Hapag, enabling the company to maintain its weekly schedule even under the extreme weather conditions of the winter months.

A preliminary peak of 59 round voyages was reached by 1873.

North German Lloyd takes the lead in passenger shipping (1858–1888)

Much like Hapag, the NORDDEUTSCHER LLOYD (NORTH GERMAN LLOYD) was born out of the initiative taken by a few farsighted men from its home port, Bremen. This applies foremostly to the driving force of Consul Hermann Henrich Meier, an experienced merchant in the US trade and shipowner, and Eduard Crüsemann with a similar professional background. H. H. Meier had already taken a leading role in providing capital for the Ocean Steam Navigation Company and since then he never lost sight of his plan for the establishment of a reliable Bremen steamship connection with the USA.

On February 20, 1857 North German Lloyd was founded by merger of four smaller joint-stock companies with an initial capital of barely 3 million Taler, after the Bremen Senate had given its consent two days earlier.

The members of the supervisory board included, apart from the Chairman H. H. Meier, quite a number of prominent members of the Bremen society such as C. Melchers, L. Delius, G. F. Grosse and J. G. Kulenkampff, names which still exist today.

Similar to Hapag, Lloyd also had difficulty in attracting sufficient starting capital. All well-known German banks, which were invited to subscribe, still refused to participate in the project of a German steamship connection with America at that time. Bremen's shipowners, therefore, had to a large extent also to rely on their own citizens for a risk partnership.

The word "Lloyd" had been synonymous with shipping since the establishment of Edward Lloyd's famous London coffee house and the later association of underwriters. With the name North German Lloyd a counterpart was to be established to the Austrian Lloyd, which had been operating from Triest since 1836. This was a clear signal that the scope of Lloyd's activities was intended to reach far beyond the Weser port.

Hapag and Lloyd, therefore, possessed almost identical operational and strategical objectives right from the beginning. This applied equally to the principle of securing the reliability of the new service by the employment of the most modern ships and by high demands in the selection and quality of their staff on board as well as ashore.

The company's first orders were for three smaller iron screw steamers to be delivered in 1857, in order to inaugurate a passenger and cargo service between Bremen and London. However, the primary purpose was the establishment of a steamship line between Bremen and New York, and orders were placed at two British ship yards for four iron screw steamers of over 2,000 tons.

On June 19, 1858 the "Bremen" opened the North Atlantic service from Bremerhaven to New York with 22 cabin and 93 steerage passengers as well as 150 tons of cargo. She arrived at New York on July 4, after a passage of fourteen and a half days and returned on July 30, with 60 passengers and 220 tons of cargo after a fast journey of only 12 days.

The other three ships, the „New York", the "Hudson" and the "Weser" set out on their maiden voyages in the second half of 1858. Thus the prospective fortnightly service could have been put into operation according to schedule. Unfortunately, however, due to a series of accidents three vessels in succession dropped out and a further five years were to pass before the intended service was firmly established.

The young, still unstable enterprise was, therefore, put to one of the severest endurance tests of its entire 125 years' history right at the beginning. The two ships that were built at Newcastle, "Hudson" and "Weser" were so badly damaged by fire and heavy weather, that they had to be sold. To make things worse, on the return voyage of the "Bremen" its crankshaft broke, so that she had to undergo repairs lasting six months.

These set-backs coincided with one of the most serious economic depressions in the United States and caused considerable unrest among the shareholders. But Consul Meier presented himself as a pillar of strength: by his calm and convincing appearance he was able to regain the confidence first of the supervisory board and then also of the A.G.M. and, as its new chairman, he was given a free hand to continue his course.

This coat of arms was carried at the bows of Lloyd's two express steamers "Bremen" and "Europa" from 1929 to 1933, combining the flags of the two nations which they served and the company's own flag. It symbolised their intimate relationship in those times, but it applies no less today.

Emigrants embark at Hamburg on a barge which takes them to the ocean-going Hapag steamer lying at anchor in the lower Elbe river.

The Hoboken berths in New York of the Bremen and Hamburg shipping lines, seen here in 1865 with North German Lloyd's "Hansa" and Hapag's "Germania" and "Bavaria" alongside.

North German Lloyd's pier and waiting halls in Bremerhaven. A railroad terminal on the quay made it possible for passengers to board the ship directly from the train.

The last hurdle to recovery came when one of the principal shareholders – the Darmstädter Bank – offered Consul Meier their Lloyd shares at an exchange rate of 28 percent for repurchase. Meier kept his nerves and accepted, as he had, fortunately, just received a sizeable amount for the sale of the "Weser". He subsequently received official approval from the general meeting for this cool and prudent decision. The US Postmaster General came to the rescue when it was agreed that British-American mail would be forwarded with the two remaining Lloyd vessels. This brought extra returns of US $ 5,000 per round trip and contributed to a moderate profit for the company in 1859.

As of March 1859 the NGL ships were making intermediate calls at Southampton both on the outward and homeward legs, and were thereby becoming serious competitors also for the British lines.

S. S. "Hudson" was replaced by the 3,000 ton "Hansa" in November 1861 and the "Weser" by the 2,750 ton "America" in May 1863. With four ships now available, a fortnightly service could be offered.

The scene was therefore set for strong and long-lasting competition between the two German carriers, Hapag and Lloyd, until their merger in 1970.

Perhaps Hapag-Lloyd would never have reached its leading position in international shipping without the ensuing competition between its two parent companies. Phases of cooperation and partnership were interrupted by phases of mutual aggressiveness, and the latter usually became costly experiences for both parties. In retrospect this development has produced a most fascinating story.

A first limited agreement on joint activity between the two companies was reached in 1861 regarding sailing dates and fares.

Four additional ships were put into service by Lloyd between 1865–67, thus enabling a weekly service. The quality of the ships was permanently improved, so that speed and comfort attracted more and more passengers to the Bremen Line:
7,000 passengers in 1859, 15,100 in 1864, 28,500 in 1866 and 33,400 in 1867.

In 1863, Lloyd acquired extensive dock facilities at Hoboken in the port of New York.

In March of 1868, Lloyd inaugurated a new line from Bremen via Le Havre and Southampton to Baltimore on a monthly basis. For this purpose, a new company called the North American Steamship Company was formed. One half of the capital was subscribed by Lloyd and the remainder by the Baltimore & Ohio Railroad, which undertook to provide the necessary pier and warehouse accommodation in Baltimore.

In the same year, a new subsidiary service from Bremen, Le Havre and Southampton to Havana and New Orleans was started.

The outbreak of the Franco-Prussian war in July 1870 forced Lloyd to suspend its North Atlantic services for several months to avoid the risk of its ships being captured by the French Navy. When in November the "Union" with over 300 passengers on board sailed from Bremen via the north of Scotland, it ran aground near Rattray Head. Her passengers and crew were saved, but the ship was a total loss. It was not before February and March 1871 that the regular services to New York, Baltimore and New Orleans could be resumed.
Soon the increase in numbers of emigrants induced Hapag and Lloyd each to dispatch extra sailings to New York in addition to their weekly services.

In July 1877 Johann G. Lohmann took over command in Bremen as President of the Board of Directors at the age of 47. He was a man of great energy who soon realised that Lloyd, although keeping in step with Hapag in their Trans-Atlantic services, had fallen behind the British lines in ship size and speed. Lohmann therefore decided to place an order for an "express" steamer that would match the best ships in international shipping. The new ship, the 4,500 ton "Elbe" capable of 16 knots, the standard speed then having been 12–13 knots, was ordered from Elder in Glasgow. During her maiden trip in 1881 she established, as intended, a new record of eight days on the route from Southampton to New York, and this fast connection soon attracted American passengers in particular. This success prompted Lloyd to place further orders for four slightly larger ships, "Werra", "Fulda", "Eider" and "Ems", which arrived in time to accommodate the new wave of German emigrants of the early eighties. According to the Company's impressive statistics for their Bremen–New York service, their carryings increased from: 27,000 passengers in 1879, to 60,000 in 1880 and 87,000 in 1881.

An early ad for Hapag's weekly steamship service from Hamburg to New York as well as its bi-weekly service to New Orleans by its port agent August Bolten, Hamburg, in January 1867.

The Hamburg port agent August Bolten advertises Hapag's new sail packet service to the New World in contemporary style: "Hamburg-American Packet Line from Hamburg to New York: these most glorious and of proven worth, copper-bottomed, three-masted packets of this line will be expedited with passengers and freight on the undermentioned days:…further particulars regarding passage and freight can be obtained from the ship broker." "Specially recommendable opportunity for cabin and steerage passengers"

The oldest surviving photo of a meeting of North German Lloyd's ship officers in the port of New York. Rings showing rank were worn on caps at the time (1875).

A North German Lloyd
advertisement dating
from 1879:
"Imperial German Mail".

Page 19

The beautiful old-fashioned
oak panelled smoking
saloon of Lloyd's express
steamer "Lahn I"
(5,700 tons, 19 knots),
commissioned in 1887.

Express steamer "Aller",
1886, ladies' lounge.

Express steamer "Aller",
1886, salon.

Three further express steamers of 5,000 tons each, "Aller", "Trave" and "Saale" were commissioned in 1885. They were built of steel and were the first North Atlantic express liners to be fitted with triple expansion engines, which gave them a speed of nearly 18 knots. The 5,700 ton "Lahn", which followed in 1887, had a trial speed of 19.5 knots, rarely exceeded even by today's modern vessels.

Two ships of 6,900 tons each, the "Spree" and "Havel", were commissioned in 1890/91, and although reaching a trial speed of 20 knots, did not live up to expectations. They were overshadowed by the four new twin-screw ships previously put into service by Hapag.

With 11 express steamers now available for the New York route, the service could be increased in 1891 to sailings three times a week from Bremen and twice-weekly from Southampton, remarked on by N.R.P. Bonsor in his book "North Atlantic Seaway" as being "probably the most outstanding long-distance service ever provided on any route".

The voyage results remained however unsatisfactory so that as of October 1891 several of the older express steamers were diverted to a new service from New York to Genoa and Naples to attract a growing number of wealthy Americans intending to visit their countries of origin or to embark on a holiday trip to the Old World and westbound in order to participate in the emigration boom from Italy and Austria-Hungarian territories to USA. Italian passenger shipping was still in its infancy then. In December 1893 Hapag followed suit with their new express steamers during the winter months and in 1894 arrangements were made by Hapag and Lloyd to operate their first joint service as the German Mediterranean Service.

In 1893, Lloyd inaugurated, in addition, a new cargo and steerage passenger line between Bremen and New York at lower tariffs than its express service, under the trade name "Roland Line".
By 1888 the Lloyd had placed itself at the top of international shipping with a package of services which had meanwhile also extended to Brazil and the River Plate (1875) and to East Asia and to Australia via the Suez Canal (1886). In March Consul H. H. Meyer retired as Chairman of the Supervisory Board after having served his company for 30 years and of whom Otto von Bismarck's characteristics of a regal merchant truly applied.

Emigrants direct the Course of transatlantic Shipping (1850–1950)

Emigration constituted by far the most important outbound traffic from Europe to the USA in the 19th Century. Together with mail it provided the basis for Hapag and Lloyd services across the Atlantic and also directed the course of technical development. On the homebound leg cabin passengers and US export cargo were predominant.

Both shipping companies owed their rapid growth to the vast numbers of Europeans who were hoping for a new successful life in America. It was certain that everyone would find a new job there — even with good pay, which was not at all the situation in Europe. A population boom had raised the number of Europeans from 140 million in 1750 to 255 million in 1850 — almost doubling the population in but a century. Germans alone increased by more than 130 % in the Nineteenth Century; from 25 million in 1800 to 65 million in 1900. Such speedy growth could hardly be absorbed by the economy, and the result was heavy unemployment. Emigration became a panacea for European ills, and as Traugott Bromme explained in his book "Rathgeber für Auswanderungslustige" (A Guide for Would-Be Emigrants): "those with no possessions, who with the support of their community are conveyed to America, can through their own diligence gain property there, rather than go under in misery and corruption, as has been the case here until now" (1846).

Emigration to the US, however, fluctuated year by year and made it all the more difficult to maintain a regular and competitive passenger service. In 1865 for example, only 58,000 Germans left for America, whereas the number suddenly jumped to 120,000 the following year.

The transition from sailing ships to steamships was a most significant factor in the development of emigration. Hapag and Lloyd were pioneers in the progress of emigration services, and their consistent high quality had a considerable bearing on shipping standards elsewhere.

The texts below explain the photos on both pages from upper left to bottom right.

The emigrant traffic via Hamburg and Bremen reached its peak at the turn of the century and during the period until 1914. The greater part of those emigrants came from Eastern and South Eastern Europe, where poverty among the masses was especially serious. Hapag built an enormous transit camp for the emigrants in Hamburg, where they were able to receive medical treatment as well as everything else they needed during the waiting periods before the ships sailed provided almost free of charge.

Medical inspection of arriving transit passengers on the premises of the transit camp near the port area.

Emigrants gathering on the square in front of the Catholic and Protestant churches, in which daily services were provided.

Shopping street in the emigrant transit camp at Hamburg.

Steerage passengers walking from the camp to the berth of the waiting river boat for transfer to the Hapag ocean steamers; a band plays farewell.

Embarkation of passengers on board of the river boat for transfer to the ocean steamer down-river.

Steerage passengers on board of the Hapag steamer "Graf Waldersee" lining up on deck for lunch.

Even when it still had sailing ships, Hapag tried to provide the kind of comfort then normally found only on steamers. On the "Borussia", red satin, gold embellished furniture and landscape drawings made the first class "bedrooms as handsome as the parlor", the second class accommodation was "no less convenient and comfortable", and the steerage passengers had a room that was an unusual eight-feet high, with "fans for ventilation".

The introduction of steamships for passenger transport shortened trips at sea by a full month, so that only two weeks instead of six were needed to cross the Atlantic. With the decrease in duration, all the other dangers and discomforts decreased as well. For a clear comparison, in 1877 2.5 % of the passengers on sailing ships died, whereas only 0.1 % of the steamship passengers died that year. In 1853, the press was already condemning sailing vessels and calling them "damned plagueships and floating coffins" and "horrors of emigration".

At a time when poor conditions and low safety standards were accepted as normal even by passengers, Hapag and Lloyd were stepping ahead and trying to upgrade their services.

Already on the first steamships technical and organisational installations, matching present day standards, were to be found. Fire extinguishers in the cargo area, free medical help, extensive ventilation, steam heaters and even electric bell systems connecting passengers cabins with stewards rooms. The first Hapag steamer, the "Borussia" was already three times as large as Hapag's last and largest sailing packet. Instead of 17-men crews, crews of initially 77 up to 1000 men on the express passenger ships of the "Imperator"-class served these larger ships. Provisions, sanitary conditions and courteous treatment, safety and speed, frequency and regularity were the key aspects with which to attract passengers, and all were considerably improved by the introduction of steamships.

Hapag and Lloyd were especially successful in drawing business on the basis of improved conditions. Competition between them as well as competition with foreign carriers, such as companies based in Liverpool, Le Havre and Antwerp, provided much of the impetus for raising standards. Although it took a number of years and hard work for Bremen and Hamburg to succeed in drawing the majority of German emigrants to their ports, outside competition was successfully overcome by both companies through foresight and careful attention to detail.

Peak emigration periods frequently resulted in a shortage of inexpensive accommodation for transit passengers. In 1892, Hapag responded to the need by converting idle ships into additional living space.

It was the year when a cholera epidemic broke out in Hamburg and the Senate of the city-state ordered a quarantine lasting several months, which brought the emigrant traffic to the United States almost entirely to a standstill. The Hapag express service had, for a while, to be redirected to Wilhelmshaven and Southampton, causing the company considerable financial losses.

Whilst the German proportion of the total European emigrants during the years 1881–1885 was still about 25 percent, in the period between 1890 and the First World War the majority was comprised of Russians, Poles, Hungarians, Austrians, Serbs, Rumanians and jews of different nationalities, who travelled overseas via Hamburg and Bremen. Mainly it had been the poorest among the poor, who arrived from Czarist Russia or the Austro-Hungarian Monarchy, due to social distress, political persecution and/or religious suppression, and who had sold their last belongings in order to pay for the costs of the railway ticket and the ship's passage to the country of their hopes.

For them the Hanseatic cities had been the last station in the Old World on their journey to their new homeland. The lodging houses in the two cities could no longer accommodate such a tremendous stream of transit passengers. There was also the danger of intrusion of epidemics, as had been manifested so dreadfully by the cholera year in Hamburg.

At the request of the Hamburg Senate, Hapag, therefore, established on an area of the America-Quay, that had been provided by the city, a camp for a total of 1,400 persons, where those foreign guests were taken care of from their arrival until their embarcation on the Transatlantic ships including free medical treatment. Apart from dormitories, day rooms with tables and benches were available, in which meals could be taken, offered at moderate prices.

When in 1900 the Hamburg port authority needed the camp area for other purposes, Hapag entrusted the German architect Georg Thielen with the creation of a small city for emigrants on an adjacent site in the Veddel district. It was to be equipped with all modern facilities so as to render life for the transit passengers as comfortable as possible. The new establishment was inaugurated in 1901 and offered space for initially 1,000 and as of 1907 up to 5,000 passengers per day with an annual throughput of between 100,000 and 500,000 travellers.

The drastic decline of the East European emigration via the German ports during the years 1892–94 as a consequence of the draconic transit restrictions, imposed by the Senate of Hamburg and the Prussian government, was threatening, much to the detriment of the German lines, to permanently divert this traffic to other European ports, the Rhine-estuary ports in particular.

Hapag and Lloyd, therefore, decided to take the law into their own hands and, as of 1895, with the German government's consent, established on the German frontiers joint controlling stations for their own account and management, in order to ensure that, by an appropriate and reasonable organisation, the great number of East European emigrants would no longer be abruptly sent back by the authorities for lack of proper documents and funds and thereby losing them as passengers. From that time both shipping companies took over the risk, which the government was no longer willing to bear, namely to return for their own account emigrants, who did not receive immigration permits in the USA, to the border of their native country. From 1884 onwards the USA began to render serious difficulties for the admission of destitute immigrants, the so-called "paupers".

The German shipping companies, at the same time, also provided an important health service with these controlling stations. Each foreign emigrant, who travelled without a valid passport and who could not present a ship's ticket of one of the licensed shipping companies in Germany, or a railway ticket to a port of embarcation, or did not possess the necessary cash to pay the full costs of the return journey, in case of being refused entry in the USA, had to report to the controlling stations. There they were registered and examined by a doctor, after having taken a bath and their clothes as well as their luggage were thoroughly disinfected. Only those transit passengers, who had received

Hapag's emigrant city located in the port of Hamburg after its extension in 1907 with direct train connection seen at the right hand corner.

Hapag's extensive New York pier facilities at Hoboken, N. J., built in 1883, comprised of initially 2 piers, 3 spacious sheds with electric lights, a duty-free warehouse and residential premises for the staff. Incoming and outgoing traffic was directed on two separate roads. During the nineties a third pier and two additional warehouses were added. These docks were, according to contemporary reports, among the most spectacular buildings in the port area of New York at the time.

a clean bill of health from the doctors, obtained a travel permit. With these sanitary measures the intrusion of contagious diseases in the ports and aboard should, as far as one could judge, be prevented.

Little by little these controlling stations were extended to all border stations of the railway trunk lines of the German Reich from Tilsit via Thorn, Posen, Ratibor up to Bingerbrück, as well as a station in Berlin for all those, who succeeded to pass the border secretly or uncontrolled.

Only by these measures was it possible to reopen the German borders to East European emigrants heading for German ports of embarcation, instead of deporting them in sealed trains, as did happen, immediately across the Western borders to the foreign competition.

The new emigrant city of the Hamburg-Amerika Line now constituted the final link in the chain of precautionary health measures, from the moment the emigrants crossed the German border until embarcation. Emigrants arrived direct in special trains or in specially reserved waggons at the camp's railroad terminal, without having to transit through the city of Hamburg. Those emigrants were thus also no longer exposed to the earlier dangers of falling victim to unscrupelous tradesmen or of being defrauded by the so-called "runners".

Here the emigrants were once again registered on arrival, their travel schedule counterchecked, like in a modern travel agency, and once again also a medical inspection took place, after everybody had taken a hot shower and their clothes and luggage were disinfected a second time after the long and tiresome journey. Persons and their relatives, who were suspected to have an infectious disease, were sent for observation to its own hospital. Sick persons were transferred to the municipal hospitals. Only after this procedure, were persons permitted to enter the actual city, where they were accommodated in attractive pavillons of four dormitories each with 22 beds, families together, singles separated by the sexes.

Each pavillon was equipped with bathrooms and toilets as well as living rooms for use during day time. Meals were served in friendly canteens and the emigrant found everything, which he needed for the ship's passage and his new life overseas at low prices in a shopping centre.

The pavillon system offered the advantage that, at the outbreak of a contagious disease, emigrants could be better isolated and thereby a broader spread of the disease prevented. It also enabled the separation of the different nationalities, ethnical groups, confessions and sects, whose cohabitation frequently gave rise to disputes. It thus happened that on a single day members of 24 confessions and sects respectively found entry in the emigrant city simultaneously.

There were also separate dining rooms for Christians and Jews. A special kitchen prepared food strictly in conformity with the Jewish ritual under supervision of a Chief Rabbi. In the center of the city a Catholic and a Protestant church provided daily services, while a separate prayer room was available for emigrants of the Jewish faith.

A band played every day in a music pavillon for the waiting passengers, since it had been the concern of the shipping company to make the long and tiresome journeys as pleasant as possible for their passengers by entertainment programs ashore and on board.

All buildings were fitted with central heating and electric lighting. The waste water and sewage were not, as was still common practice at that time, led unfiltered into the Elbe, but according to most modern environmental principles had first been processed and then chemically cleaned.

"With their neat lodgings, churches and gardens they constituted a friendly and spacious colony; it is, so to speak, a small town of its own", concluded the Association of Hamburg Architects and Engineers in its 2-volume work on "Hamburg and its buildings" in 1914. After completion Hapag's Emigrant Halls" were considered exemplary for the accommodation of emigrants. A model was awarded the grand prix at the World Exhibition in Paris in 1900.

Most of the emigrants were poverty-stricken and had very little money to pay for the stopovers, which sometimes lasted for up to a week. Hapag and Lloyd — since 1907 the Bremen shipping company also built emigrant halls, although on a smaller scale — pursued apart from the described sanatory also humanitarian aims.

Thus the price for lodgings, food, bath, desinfection and medical treatment including medicine in the Hamburg Emigrant Halls amounted to

1 Mark per day. Children were charged half-price and also this very low price was only charged to those, who were in a position to pay, while destitutes or persons who possessed only small funds were fed free of charge often for weeks during the illness of a family member. Consequently, during a period of five years of the 285,000 transit passengers, who were accommodated in the emigrant city, 71,300 persons, or about 25 percent, did not pay anything.

In relation to the miserable conditions under which emigrants had been transported from a number of European ports in former times, the social services provided by the two German lines to those waiting passengers almost free of charge, was certainly unique in world ocean transport.

Not without pride Hapag remarked in a brochure about its "Emigrant Halls" that since their existence not a single case of infectious disease had broken out during the voyages on one of the emigrant ships which had sailed from Hamburg.

Tenders brought the passengers and emigrants from Hamburg to Brunshausen aboard the express steamers, which laid at anchor there on the lower Elbe river due to insufficient fairway depth at the turn of the century.

Passengers of the nineties on board of an overseas steamer with course America.

Ballin takes command in Hamburg (1886)

During Hapag's first 25 years of growth and prosperity under the capable leadership of Godeffroy, the foundation was laid for the worldwide expansion in the Ballin era. This first phase was followed, and indeed overshadowed, by an interim of 12 years of depression and cut-throat competition. During this period both companies had to experience for the first time that competition in ocean shipping is not always stimulating and innovative but can also be most destructive and destabilizing for those involved.

Many new North Atlantic lines sprang up during the boom years of 1871–73. One of the most ambitious had been the Adler Line, which, in 1873, started a service from Hamburg to New York in direct competition with Hapag. This newcomer got its financial backing from the Hamburg shipping companies Laeisz and Sloman as well as from Berlin banks including the Deutsche Bank. The capital stock of the new company amounted to 12 m Thaler, while that of Hapag was only 10.5 m. Adler engaged seven new steamers of equal size and speed (2,300 dwt, 13 knots), and immediately tried to operate a weekly service like its established competitor. Soon after this line started operations, a severe worldwide recession set in that lasted until 1879 and sharply reduced the cargo flow as well as the stream of emigrants. This prompted the newcomer to drastically reduce not only freight rates, but also steerage fares. Hapag and Lloyd had no choice but to follow suit. Although this rate war only lasted a year and a half, it was nevertheless devastating in its financial consequences. Hapag suffered a loss of 1.8 m Mark in 1874, while in the previous year a profit of 2.7 m was achieved. Adler Line could not hold out this severe competition. An arrangement was, therefore, agreed upon, in which Hapag took over Adler's six ocean vessels, together with its facilities and stores before the line was liquidated in 1875. An arrangement was agreed upon, in which Hapag took over Adler's six ocean vessels. The seventh vessel had been wrecked on the Scilly Islands with very heavy loss of life.

Although this transaction enabled Hapag to return rates and fares quickly to a profitable level, the financial burden of the accumulated capital and extra tonnage brought the company to the brink of bankrupcy. Time and again, in the course of the history of both companies, such mergers proved most dangerous and in this case Hapag experienced four consecutive years in which no dividends could be paid, while in 1876 a deficit of almost 3.5 m marks was recorded. Once again Godeffroy exhibited his excellent leadership by inducing the A.G.M. to reduce the capital by one third and to issue new and more favorable debentures. This saved the company, and one year later a first dividend of 7 % could be granted again.

Four years after Hapag had recovered from these heavy losses, another strong competitor in Hamburg started a direct service to New York. In June of 1881, Edward Carr began with two cargo steamers, gradually increasing to five ships with accommodation for 600 steerage passengers each. The general agent and actual promoter of this new service was the 24 year-old Albert Ballin, who within a few years had built up a considerable reputation for his father's firm, Morris & Co., an emigrant agency canvassing for British Trans-Atlantic lines.

Ballin was the youngest of nine children of the Jewish merchant Samuel Joel Ballin, who was married to a woman from Hamburg. He had immigrated from Denmark to Hamburg in 1830 and later started his own business. It was, however the son who, due to his outstanding entrepreneurial skills, achieved admission into the ranks of Hamburg's high society.

Until then he had been booking passages for the indirect business, in which steerage passengers were ferried from Hamburg to Liverpool or Southampton for transfer to the Atlantic terminals. At that time more than one third of European emigrants embarking from Hamburg used this indirect route, which significantly cut into the business of direct lines.

Upon Ballin's suggestion, Edward Carr, a nephew of Hamburg's prominent shipowner Robert M. Sloman jr., had the upperdecks of the two steamships on order fitted with accommodation for emigrants. Ballin had guaranteed to fully utilize the passenger space of the two vessels at a passage fare of 82 Mark per head to New York. In comparison, Hapag charged then 120 Mark for a steerage passage. Ballin even offered to pay Carr a penalty of 20 Mark for each unutilised space.

Albert Ballin, Chairman of Hamburg-America Line from 1886 to 1918 used to say "Mein Feld ist die Welt" (The world is my domain). He built up the company to be the world's largest shipping line. But he was also recognized by his competitors as the great organizer and architect of the trans-atlantic passenger and cargo conference system constituting the crucial prerequisite for trade stability that lasted for more than 20 years to the benefit of transport users and suppliers.

The operational costs of the ordinary freight liners without the expensive cabin outfit were, of course, much lower than of the fast packet steamers. This gave him a considerable margin below the official passenger fares, while still permitting a reasonable profit. Apart from the cheaper fare the steerage passengers were also permitted to move freely all over the ship instead of being cramped into a small section in the front during the voyage.

He was soon so successful that Hapag and Lloyd were forced to lower their tariffs for both directions, which in turn, obliged the Carr Line to follow suit. By 1885, the return fare from New York had been worked down from the original conference level of US$ 30.00 to US$ 6.00, forcing both sides to negotiate a settlement.

By then, Carr was also prepared to offer his vessels for sale to Hapag, but as they could not agree on the price, negotiations dragged on until March of 1886. Hapag finally gave in, but only to learn that Ballin had meanwhile arranged for the Carr Line to merge with Sloman's "America Line" under the new trade name "Union Line". The combined tonnage of the merged lines was approaching Hapag's capacity on this route. This new situation considerably strengthened the bargaining power of Hapag's opponents. In sober recognition of their financial limitations, Ballin proposed, however, to pool the sailings of the Union-Line with those of the Hapag, and finally an agreement was reached. Hapag was to be in charge of passenger bookings for both lines and would guarantee the Union a share of at least 25 % of the passengers. More importantly, Hapag offered Ballin a five year contract to serve as head of its passenger department. His great professional qualities, organizational skills and creative genius had already been amply displayed while conducting this outsider service, and without hesitation he immediately set to work to recoup the losses Hapag had incurred during the previous decade.

On January 1, 1885, Hapag had already taken over from August Bolten, its exclusive passenger agent in Hamburg since its foundation, booking of passengers under its own management.

Ballin's intimate knowledge of the agency structure on the Continent as well as his good contacts to the British lines soon proved to be invaluable assets for his future tasks. One of his first steps was to reduce the British

influence on the Hamburg passenger spot market. The market power of the emigrant agencies in the steerage bookings sometimes exceeded that of the carriers, and with their high provisions they had become "war profiteers" in the competitive struggles.

Ballin fully recognized that Hapag's damaging competitive struggle with the Adler and Carr Line in quick succession during the past decade, had enabled its strongest rival Lloyd to stabilize its position in the North Atlantic with its superior express service. He was determined that Hapag should regain its leading position as quickly as possible and convinced the board that a new service with express steamers would be the only way to meet Bremen's powerful challenge. For that purpose the company's capital was raised by five million marks with an additional ten million in debentures in 1887.

An initial controversy only arose between Ballin and the Chairman of the supervisory board Carl Laeisz when dealing with the shareholders. His successor of a few years later recorded it in his memoirs:

"… although Ballin urged with all his persuasiveness the resumption of payments of dividends, Laeisz maintained, in view of the depleted financial status of the company, with great composure his veto. When in a general meeting a shareholder peremptorily demanded payment of a dividend, Laeisz replied as chairman with the classical remark: 'According to paragraph 1 of our statutes the purpose of our company is the running of a shipping company and not the distribution of dividends.'"

Still in the same year, orders were placed for two twin-screw steamers of over 7,000 grt each, one with the British yard Laird of Birkenhead, and the other for the first time with a German yard, Vulcan of Stettin. Credit went to the then Prince William, who later became Emperor William II, who through Chancellor von Bismarck's mediation submitted a memorandum to Hapag, in which he referred to the efficiency and capability of the Stettin yard, with the request, to include them in future shipbuilding orders.

Kurt Himer reported about this interesting high-ranking intervention: "Hapag caught on this suggestion and did very well by it; indeed it became the promoter of a magnificant development of German shipbuilding to performances, which in no way fell short of those of the British shipbuilding

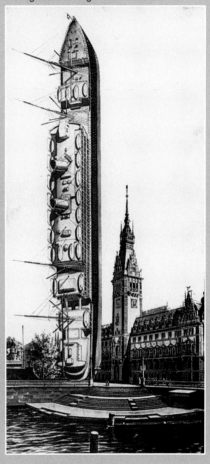

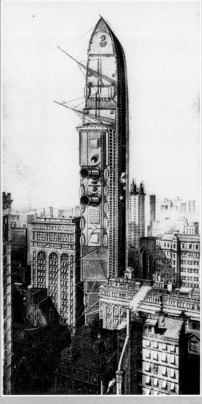

Hapag's S. S. "Amerika" and "Kaiserin Auguste Victoria" of 22/24,500 grt of 1905/06 represented a new class of spacious and luxurious express steamers that had the double length of Hamburg's town hall and of the Park Row building at New York representing at the turn of the century with its 30 stories the highest building in Manhattan.

The 7,661 grt "Auguste Victoria" leaving New York. This vessel and the "Columbia" (7,241 grt) were the first twin-screw express steamers operated by Hapag. They went into service in 1889.

The five star restaurant "Ritz-Carlton" on board of "Kaiserin Auguste Victoria" (24,580 grt) where passengers could entertain their guests à la carte round the clock. She went into service in 1906.

Lounge in the first class of express-steamer "Kaiserin Auguste Victoria".

industry, and at times even surpassed them."

The Stettin-built "Augusta Victoria" — named after the young German Emperor's wife — was the first to be completed and represented by far the biggest ship so far delivered by any German shipyard. "It belied the doubts that had existed in many minds as to the advisability of entrusting such an important contract to a German shipyard."

Both ships fully met the Company's high expectations and performed their maiden voyages in 1889 in the record time of about seven days from Southampton to New York. Southampton was called at regularly again after a lapse of 20 years. The final pair, enabling Hapag to offer a weekly express service, the 8,200 ton "Normannia" (by Fairfield of Glasgow) and the "Fürst Bismarck" (by Vulkan of Stettin) followed in 1890—91. The latter was able to set a new record in completing the run from Southampton to New York of approximately 3,100 miles in 6 days, 14 hours, 7 minutes at an average speed of 19.5 knots.

The sportsmanlike Americans in particular greeted these new Hapag vessels with enthusiasm. On "Augusta Victoria's" arrival on her maiden voyage at New York more than 30,000 visitors lined up to come on board, in order, as a publication of that year put it, "to have a look at the miracle ship and to express full appreciation of its performance and outfitting". But people in their home port of Hamburg were excited too, when the news broke that the German-built ships had set up an all-time record for the Southampton — New York route on their maiden voyages.

These yacht-like, three-funnelled steamers were 460 feet long, and their 13,000 hp engines used up 4,800 tons of coal per voyage, the equivalent of 240 railway cars.

The quartet was thus able to perform round voyages from Hamburg to New York via Southampton and back at four-weekly intervals including docking, which is exactly the calculated performance of our present weekly container service in the North Atlantic trade!

The US Postmaster General recorded that in 1890—91 the "Fürst Bismarck" was by far the fastest of all ships in delivering US mail to England with an average of 169.4 hours, followed by "Columbia" (173.6 hours) and "Normannia" (177.5 hours).

Hapag also ranged first in the immigration statistics in the transport of steerage passengers in that peak year of 1891.

With this new express service that was performed with the greatest punctuality, Hapag was offering, with the exception of the three winter months, sailings from Hamburg to New York every Thursday with express steamers, every Sunday with mail liners, and each Wednesday with a Carr-Union emigrant steamer at cheaper fares.

In Hapag's annual report of February, 1889 we find the following remarkable notice on the appointment of Carl Schurz as its American general representative:

"The Company was pleased to have been in a position to announce on the day of the launching of the 'Augusta Victoria' that for the newly created position of President of the Hamburg America Line (America) Incorporated, with his residence in New York, we have been able to secure the services of the former Secretary of the Interior and Senator of the United States, Karl Schurz. We, as Germans, can count ourselves fortunate to have gained the talents and abilities, as well as the statesmanlike and commercial experience of our renowned countryman for the fostering of relationships and dealings between our two nations."

Schurz held that position until 1892.

In recognition of Ballin's eminent leadership he was appointed a member of the Board of Directors in 1888.

During the years to follow Ballin was able to stabilize and expand Hapag's activities on a worldwide basis. From the moment Ballin joined the company its fortunes for the next three decades were first of all the product of his own genius and initiatives. Already during the first decade of his activities he consistently modernised and enlarged the fleet of passenger and cargo liners and with this new and economical tonnage of top design added 15 new routes to the company's liner services.

But Ballin was also a master in crisis management. When in August 1892 the cholera epidemic broke out in Hamburg, steerage passenger traffic immediately came to a complete standstill for almost one and a half years, due to an overreaction by the Hamburg public authorities, who ignored the fact that this epidemic was not imported by Russian emigrants,

but was caused by the unfiltered municipal water supply. Ballin tried to contain the damage thereby inflicted to a minimum by immediately switching the turn around of the express steamships from Hamburg to Southampton and by contracting, as a precautionary measure, with Lloyd and the Oldenburg government authorities a possible transfer of the operational centre to Bremen and the despatch of the ships from the Weser port Nordenham, situated opposite of Bremerhaven. Piers and warehouses had already been leased in the Oldenburg port and steamers of the West Indies service were in fact expedited from that port then.

In the social area a disability, widow and orphan pension fund was established for Hapag employees. It was the predecessor of Hapag-Lloyd's present pension and retirement funds. When Ballin presented the budget for the passenger business to the supervisory board in 1896, the chairman retorted in variation of a word that was dropped in the Prussian Diet that the supervisory board "will appropriate this ministry each cent". The spirit of that time even among the keenest competitors is reflected in a congratulatory telegram on the occasion of Hapag's fiftieth anniversary on May 27th, 1897, by Cunard's Chairman, Lord Inverclyde, who had been invited to attend:

"... I have the greatest admiration for the diligence and enterprising style

with which your company has been led in the past years.

You were the first to give the travelling public a rapid and reliable transport between the two great continents of the world, in that you created a regular service by twin-screw steamers offering high speeds and unsurpassed accommodation.

You gave the shipping world a model of economy with the shipment of goods in vessels of much increased tonnage and corresponding profitability, an example that other nations have quickly followed to their own great advantage.

Moreover, your company has satisfied a deep-seated desire, in that you provided a most comfortable and well conceived opportunity for scenic travel, of general interest for the young as well as the old, in that you have now made such trips, that in the past brought difficulties and discomforts, as comfortable as a normal train ride.

You have achieved this, not through artificial means such as government subsidies, but rather by anticipating and responding to the wishes of passengers and businessmen, and no one, no matter of what nationality, can in the light of such facts refrain from praising the foresight, the sagacity and the skill with which such great results have been achieved in such short time, as the management of the Hamburg-American Line has done ..."

Hapag and Lloyd began the era of pleasure cruises (1890/91)

Pleasure-cruising yacht "Prinzessin Victoria Luise" of 4,400 grt built in 1900 for Hamburg-America Line, was the first purpose-built cruising liner in the world — inaugurating the era of high standard ocean-going tourism.

Hapag's cruising liner SS. "Cleveland" calling on its round-the-world cruise during the world exhibition at San Francisco in February 1910, where more than 20,000 visitors came on board to take a personal glimpse of this beautiful ship.

Cabin passengers playing a round of ring toss on deck of a Hapag express steamer at the turn of the Century.

Although during the 1880ies British and Norwegian coastal steamers began to operate trips to the Norwegian Fjords during the summer months, these ships could not offer the high comfort which became a characteristical feature of modern ocean cruising and with their excursions of a few days could be considered as forerunners at best.

In June/July 1890 Lloyd was the first to offer a pleasure cruise with the express steamer "Kaiser Wilhelm II" from Bremerhaven to Norway with 215 passengers on board, combined with land excursions to special points of interest. Although this pioneer trip proved a great success, it was Hapag that in the following year introduced cruising for pleasure on a regular schedule, thereby expanding the function of ocean shipping beyond passenger transport and goods services to the new area of tourism for pure pleasure and recreation as an end in itself.

On January 22, 1891 Hapag began its cruising program with the "Augusta Victoria", which sailed with 240 passengers, 49 of whom were foreigners from ten countries, from Cuxhaven and Southampton to the Mediterranean on a round trip lasting 53 days with organised land excursions.

Part of the motives behind these cruises was to ensure business for the express steamers during the winter, when emigration abated and they were normally laid up. But the great success of this first luxury cruise in history, in which Ballin and his wife personally took part, encouraged Hapag to develop cruising all the year round as a new business enterprise.

The hugh express steamers with their high-powered engines soon proved too expensive and also in their dimensions unsuitable, since only a strictly limited number of 1st-class passengers were accepted. Hapag, therefore, ordered its first purpose-built cruise liner from Blohm & Voss, Hamburg, in 1900. The 4,400 ton "Prinzessin Victoria Luise", named after the German emperor's daughter, embarked upon her maiden voyage in January 1901 from Hamburg to New York, from where she proceeded with a great number of American cruise passengers to the Caribbean for several weeks. Cruises followed to the Mediterranean and the Black Sea, during the summer to the British Isles as well as to Norway up to Spitzbergen and in the autumn to capitals in the Baltic.

The twin-screw ship with a speed of 15 knots looked in her external silhouette like a luxury yacht. Her spacious and elegant cabins for 180 passengers in the 1st class, attended by a crew of 160, were exclusively fitted with detached single or double beds instead of the usual berths. The dining room, lounges and promenade decks were tastefully decorated in the style of the Art Nouveau, creating the proper atmosphere for such leisure trips.

A second cruise vessel, the 3,600 ton "Meteor", was delivered in 1904 with space for 300 passengers and a crew of 150, with a speed of 12 knots. Her outfit was similar, although of a more moderate luxury so that in combination with shorter voyages cruise fares could be offered at reduced levels. This ship soon also acquired great popularity.

With the combination of land and ocean trips, to which soon also air traffic had to be added, the scope of these activities went far beyond the capabilities of the former booking agents. Already for the grand Orient trip of the "Prinzessin Victoria Luise" in 1901 the prominent British firm Cook & Son had been entrusted with catering and the organisation of the land excursions.

On January 1, 1905 Hamburg-America Line took over the oldest and most respectable German travel bureau "Carl Stangens Reisebüro" in Berlin. For one generation or 36 years respectively, Carl Stangen was considered the travel marshal of the German nation. Due to old age, he decided to transfer his excellent organisation to Hapag with its worldwide traffic connections. It was renamed in "Reisebüro der Hamburg-Amerika Linie" with a stock capital of 600,000 Mark, and its new representative main office at "Unter den Linden" No. 8 in Berlin commenced business on October 1, 1905. One month later Hapag had already opened 20 additional offices in Europe, among others in Copenhagen, Brussels, Paris, Lucern, Zurich and Warsaw.

The scope of the activities of these travel bureaus already extended almost to the total range of the Hapag-Lloyd Reisebüro GmbH of today, namely

"to offer its services to the travellers and to take all the small and yet so important and often so arduous burdens from their shoulders, which are inherent with travelling but also tiresome, if no practical expert guide supervises them." The new age of ocean cruising only obtained its successful organisational base through the foundation of these travel bureaus.

Rivalry between the two German companies for the first place in passenger shipping was keen, which quickly extended also to the cruising sector. These cruises opened up for European and American tourists many new exotic places and a few years later were also extended to round-the-world trips. When Hapag's "Cleveland" stopped in San Francisco on her round the world cruise in 1910, 20,000 people came to visit her while in port.

The Ocean Runners (1889–1914)

The most desired trophy for the fastest ship on the Atlantic was the "Blue Ribbon". It was a prized possession for liners with a passenger service, since claim to the title brought immediate renown — and thus passengers — to the company with the record breaking ship. The express steamer era was already in the second decade when the express steamer "Kaiser Wilhelm der Große" built by Vulcan of Stettin for North German Lloyd scored a new record on her maiden voyage in 1897. It was the "ship of the decade" not only in speed but also with regard to its superb interior passenger accommodation. Spurring on the competition between the large North-Atlantic lines, particularly between Hapag, Lloyd, Cunard and White Star, the Blue Ribbon received for its holder a symbolic character, for which a few well-funded shipping companies spent huge sums of money to produce the largest, fastest and most luxurious ships in efforts to gain instant public acclaim. Trade with America seemed especially promising, and many companies considered innovation and superlatives in service a realistic economic risk. Never before had shipping taken such strides in development.

Lloyd's claim to the fastest crossing of the Atlantic was lost in 1900, when Hapag commissioned the "Deutschland". Only since that date did the title Blue Ribbon find international acceptance. The word was taken from the highest British decoration, the order of the garter and its colour.

By 1903, the four fastest ships in the World – 3 Lloyd and 1 Hapag passenger liner – carried the German flag; by this time British shipping circles, above all the British Admiralty, felt to be challenged in their national pride. In order not to be relegated as the leading shipping nation to the second place, the Cunard Line with the aid of substantial government funds and after several years of intensive research and development commissioned its two express steamers "Lusitania" and "Mauretania" in autumn 1907. Hapag's "Deutschland" and Lloyd's "Kaiser Wilhelm II" proved no match for these new vessels, in view of their superior size of 30,000 grt propelled by quadruple-screws, and indeed the "Mauretania" held the Blue Ribbon for twenty-two years, until 1929 when Lloyd regained the title with her new "Bremen".

Hapag had meanwhile decided to step out of the heat of the race. After the "Deutschland" with her tremendous and completely unremunerative fuel consumption, Ballin decided that speed should be a lesser priority, and instead comfort and spaciousness became the primary goals. The Hapag philosophy was that "the passengers should be so comfortable that an extra day of travel would rather be a welcome addition".

The prototypes of this new category of ships were the 22,000 ton "Amerika" built by Harland & Wolff in 1905 and the 24,600 ton "Kaiserin Auguste Victoria" built by Vulcan of Stettin in 1906.

At the height of Hapag's success, Albert Ballin commissioned three ships to outdo all others. In 1912, the "Imperator", in 1914 the "Vaterland" and later the "Bismarck" awed the world with their impressive silhouettes and splendid interiors.

All aspects of these ships were offered in superlative measures, and they represented a culmination of shipbuilding knowledge which was not to be surpassed for quite some time to come. Hapag's first and only Blue Ribbon winner, the "Deutschland", was only one third the size of the "Imperator", and overall the "Imperator" class vessels far outclassed previous vessels.

The tremendous size of the "Imperator" class (of 55,000 grt) meant new heights and widths in shipping architecture. The peak of the ballroom ceiling was hardly matched by any room on land. More impressive was the fact that there were no supporting co-

A meeting of the members of the North-Atlantic Steamship Lines Association, at Cologne, in 1902. The founder Albert Ballin in the centre right behind the carafe. Dr. Wiegand (Lloyd) on his left (from viewer). Member Lines: Hapag (Hamburg), Union-Line (Hamburg), Lloyd (Bremen), Holland-America Line (Rotterdam), Red Star Line (Antwerp), CGT (Le Havre).

North German Lloyd in strong competition with Hapag placed at the turn of the century a total of four four-funnel express-steamers into the North Atlantic service, three of which "Kaiser Wilhelm der Große", "Kronprinz Wilhelm" and "Kaiser

Wilhelm II" were "Blue Ribbon" winners in 1897, 1902 and 1904 respectively. This famous quartet as seen on this Lloyd poster was the culmination of pre-World-War-I passenger service of this company, placing Lloyd into first rank of world's passenger lines.

lumns in the middle; a feat never before achieved anywhere else. The ballroom was also surrounded by huge dining rooms segregated by class, a smoking room, a ladies' room, a five star Ritz-Carlton Restaurant, where one could dine with friends "à la carte" round the clock. There were, in addition, an indoor swimming pool in old Pompeian style, as well as fitness rooms and rooms for games and entertainment.

Safety was of primary concern, and in this area the "Imperator" class vessels excelled as well. Just to mention a few of the innovations, all three ships were equipped with a double bottom, a collision bulkhead, several traverse and longitudinal bulkheads, as well as with a double skin, extending well above the waterline, securing the ship's interior against leakage after a collision. In case of serious damage, all watertight doors could be shut automatically from the bridge, so that an eventual inrush of seawater could be confined to the immediately affected sections. In addition, eighty-three large lifeboats with improved outfitting, over four times the number carried on the "Titanic", offered sufficient space and reserve capacity to accommodate the total of 5,100 passengers and crew.

Smoke detectors in the cargo holds and passenger accommodations would immediately signal the outbreak of fire to the bridge enabling the ship's command to initiate fire fighting measures. Fire precautions were expanded with a pipe system that could pump steam into every single room, and in addition, fireproof material had been used to build the interior walls.

Flume tanks filled with seawater, through a sophisticated system, reduced the rolling of the ship in heavy weather. A radiotelegraph with a range of 1500 miles greatly improved communications both for the command and passengers. The "Imperator" was also the first ship to be equipped with a gyrocompass.

With completion of the "Bismarck" scheduled for March/April 1915, a weekly express service of the three 50,000 ton liners between Hamburg, Cherbourg, Southampton and New York was to be established. The outbreak of the First World War prevented the realisation of these magnificant plans and the "Bismarck" was not actually completed until after the war in March 1922, when she sailed as "Majestic" for the Wite Star Line.

The masterpiece of a great diplomat: The refined network of transatlantic liner conferences and pools[1] (1892–1914)

Ballin was not only a great organizer but also a genius in diplomacy with the rare gift of bringing even the toughest opponent to the negotiating table and convincing him that a reasonable compromise was in most cases more rewarding than a fight. He was only too aware that in ocean transport rate wars would only produce losers among the participants, except for the agents – the "war profiteers" – whose commissions usually rose. One of his first moves when taking command in Hamburg was, therefore, to visit the North German Lloyd at Bremen in order to prepare the ground for closer cooperation or, at least, for a better climate between the two rivals.

Building the finest and most sophisticated fleet in the world was of no use, if in the trades where these ships were to operate, freights and passenger fares were so low as to be unprofitable. This was exactly what had happened in the Hamburg-New York trade a few years earlier. From the order books of the shipyards it was evident that within a few years there would be an overcapacity of express steamers. Therefore, Ballin felt that the time was appropriate for bringing the principal liner companies into agreement on the rules of the game.

In a note that Ballin presented in 1886 to the Continental lines, he proposed a Conference Pool for steerage traffic. According to his ideas the traffic share for each participant should be based year by year on the past performance of the preceding five years with due regard to the tonnage employed by each line. A standard fare would be fixed as well as a standard commission. Those lines like Lloyd, that exclusively engaged express steamers, would be free to charge up to a certain amount extra in order to cover their higher costs. Those lines claiming lower rates, but not exceeding a certain figure, were free to do so for their own accounts, but had to contribute to the pool with the full fares.

The basic principles which Ballin's pool idea implied – and they appear

no less captivating today – were the allocation of certain shares of the total conference trade based on the actual past performance while at the same time keeping them flexible by considering the tonnage employed. Equally modern, and much more convincing than the mechanism of "independent action" practised nowadays under the US regulation, was the possibility of differentiating the tariff according to the different qualities of service. This was a truly competitive device without the destabilising effect of secret or open rebating.

A separate opinion of an American railway expert about pooling was annexed to Ballin's note. It stated that it would be better for US inland traffic if ocean lines maintained reasonable and stable rates without offering any party special preferences. Such stable rates would free US trade from the element of insecurity created by fluctuating rates which was detrimental to the legitimate trade. A mutual allocation of ship space and revenues would be the best means for achieving this aim. Also, the US railways would not have had any better device to raise the economy of their lines after their cut-throat competitive struggles. Their central organization of rail traffic was to consist of 40 railways, and traffic was to be allocated from more than 100 terminals to an equal number of destinations.

For steamship lines, according to the American expert, the following would be necessary:

1. to fix rates and shares of the individual lines;
2. to recognize differences in the quality of transportation by means of differential rates;
3. to establish an arbitration machinery for settling disputes;
4. to establish a central bureau for statistics and division of trade;
5. to distribute traffic and revenues.

The noblest principle, however, should be: to live and let live.

Negotiations about the actual shares and terms took several years but in 1892 the pool was finally agreed upon and implemented under the name North Atlantic Steamship Lines Association (Nordatlantischer Dampfer-Linien-Verband). A share of 14 % of the Continental traffic was originally reserved for the British lines, which in that year were, however, not yet prepared to join.

The head of Lloyd's passenger department, Heinrich Peters, became the

secretary for this pooling agreement. He was one of the chief promoters and the man whose proposals broke the deadlock.

This revolutionary agreement lasted for more than 20 years and in the latter half included almost all principal lines from the Continent, Scandinavia, the UK, and the Mediterranean. Only one major carrier, the Cunard Line, decided to remain independent, newly strengthened by a huge government loan at 2¾ percent interest rate based on a 20 years' contract. In 1904 this line started a tough and for both sides unrewarding rate war, which continued for four years.

Apart from this interim period, the pool worked to the full satisfaction of all participants and greatly contributed to the stabilization and expansion of the European-US trade. A few years later it was extended to include the cargo and cabin (1st and 2nd class) traffic.

Considerable attention was dedicated to the arbitration machinery. The conference agreement including arbitration proceedings were based on German Law. As no national German Civil Law was in existence then, that of Cologne was to apply, since it was there that not only the pool had been created, but also all important meetings of the Continental lines had taken place. The chairman, and in his absence the Deputy chairman of the board of the Bar Association of Cologne was to act as arbiter. His verdict was accepted as final.

The level of confidence and high standing, which Ballin acquired as the architect of this tremendous contractual work, also among the foreign lines is highlighted by the fact that the British lines, after their entry, refused to participate in pool and conference meetings, if Ballin was not in the chair.

When in 1911 the US Administration sued the Conference on the charge of violating the domestic Sherman antitrust law of 1890, it was rejected by the Federal District Court for the Southern District of New York on November 9, 1914. In its verdict it is stated among others:

..."that the attacked agreement and the acts of the parties under it do not fall under the regulations of this act and that the reasoning of the government in this respect is unfounded" and it continues:

"The Federal court has arrived at its conclusion based on the opinion, which it has formed about the nature

[1] see under definitions on page 81.

and character of ocean transport, with which this agreement is concerned; the grievance that has existed in this trade and which to eliminate it has been the purpose of the agreement; the practice of the trading world in the treatment of the steerage transport in the past; the advantage that was gained for the trade by the execution of this agreement; the reflecting light that was cast on aim and purpose of same by the reasonable rates which in its execution had been applied and many other conditions which the agreement produced as a result and which led to an improvement of the steerage transport, as well as its ensueing benefits for the security, the comfort and the health of millions of human beings, who travel in tween-decks, to which traffic class the agreement referred to exlusively."

The Morgan Trust and its far reaching implications (1902)

For two of the large sections of Trans-Atlantic shipping – steerage traffic and cargo – the great North American Conference Pool accomplished its task of stabilizing the trade for the duration of 20 years, thus successfully providing the basis for profitability by preventing a waste of resources. Lines came to realize that the engagement of additional tonnage could only be advantageous, if it met the actual requirements of the trade and if the need could be convincingly demonstrated when applying for a higher pool share. This induced members to restrict their liner policy to the employment of a competitive and economical volume of tonnage.

Unfortunately, this did not apply to the third section, namely cabin traffic. In this branch of Transatlantic shipping, the pool only regulated prices and their differentiation according to the quality of the steamers employed, but it never extended to an allocation of shares in spite of numerous efforts over the years. This inevitably led to a tendency to try to surpass each other in speed and comfort of passenger transport, so as to attract a maximum of passengers. The result was that steamers of highest quality were to offer high frequency services throughout the year, but collectively achieved a most unsatisfactory capacity utilization for the greater part of the year, especially during the winter months.

In an interview in 1902, Ballin estimated that this overcapacity would cause the lines unnecessary costs of at least 50 million marks a year. The desire to end this deplorable situation was one of the reasons for the creation of the Morgan trust, and the other reason was to intensify European-American cooperation. Ballin was one of the early sponsors of such a cooperation in clear recognition of the growing significance of the foreign trade between the two Continents. He was supported by his friend, the head of the British shipyard Harland & Wolff in Belfast, William James Pirrie, who wanted to prevent a merger of the American owned Atlantic Transport Company with the British Leyland Line.

The United States shipping industry, beset by high construction and operation costs, fell into decay in the second half of the nineteenth century. American investment in European lines, however, was extensive, and many foreign shipping lines were controlled by US investors. The desirability of greater American participation in world shipping had been repeatedly expressed by US business leaders and by members of Congress, but without much effect.

Ensuing negotiations upon Ballin's initiative between the Atlantic Transport Company and Hapag for a joint venture failed at the last moment because Hapag's Supervisory Board considered the intended sharing of capital between the two companies as too risky, much to Ballin's annoyance.

These endeavours were quickly overtaken by events, when it became known that the American banker J. Pierpont Morgan together with other powerful American companies was about to acquire the newly established Leyland Group together with White Star, Atlantic Transport, Dominian, American Line and the Belgian Red Star Line. The combined total of their 430,000 grt surpassed the combined tonnage of Hapag and Lloyd employed in the U.S. trades at that time.

Even more dangerous were the prospects of Mr. Morgan trying to combine this powerful fleet with the major US railway lines serving the US Atlantic ports, in order to conclude by means of preferential tariffs and rebates exclusive patronage contracts. The implication of achieving such exclusive rights was that European steamship lines would be cut off from US inland transport. It was estimated that of the total cargo traffic eastbound

from North Atlantic ports destined for Europe, about 70 % originated from inland railway terminals. It was also conceivable that Morgan might attempt to buy up a controlling interest in the Hamburg-American Line and/or North German Lloyd.

In the United States at that time the US government seemed prepared to strengthen US merchant shipping by granting subsidies to US flag carriers. Mr. Morgan was obviously hoping that this combination would enable him to qualify for such subsidies. Ballin fully recognized the deadly danger for the two German flag lines, if they were unable to become associated partners with this new alliance, while still maintaining their corporate independence and identity. With the approval of the German Emperor, Ballin was empowered to start negotiations with Mr. Morgan, who in turn authorized Lord Pirrie to lead these talks on his behalf, a major shareholder of White Star Line.

Once again Ballin's excellent connections let him play all the trumps. In spite of being urged by patriotic circles, he had refused to order Hapag's ships exclusively with German ship yards. Instead he had reserved a helling permanently, on commission basis, with the British yard Harland & Wolff at Belfast, so that he had shipbuilding capacity available at any time and, in addition, got an excellent overview about the state of technical development in both countries, apart from all the political advantages which this arrangement implied. This constellation permitted him to negotiate from a position of strength.

Early in 1902, the negotiations came to a positive conclusion, and with participation of Dr. Wiegand, Lloyd's Executive President, resulted in the formation of the International Mercantile Marine Company (I.M.M.Co.). The originally intended exchange of shares between the 3 companies (I.M.M.Co., Hapag and Lloyd) had been substituted by an I.M.M.Co. guarantee of a six percent dividend for each German line in return for a share of any of their dividends exceeding that figure.

For the duration of this agreement until 1911 Hapag, owing to its prospering development resulting in an average dividend of 7.2 per cent, had to pay a total of one and a half million marks to I.M.M.Co., but this was a small amount in comparison to the financial risks involved, if such an amicable arrangement hat not been reached.

With ordering the three giant ships of the "Imperator" class in 1910 Albert Ballin was to set new standards for passenger shipbuilding and shipping in which no longer speed but comfort for the passengers was to take first priority.

The view of the 5-star restaurant "Ritz-Carlton" of the "Imperator", in which passengers could eat à la carte round the clock, gives an impression of the generosity of space that was displayed in its revolutionary architecture of the time.

The "Imperator" was also the first ship that offered passengers a swimming-pool for recreation, looking almost like a bath of the ancient Roman Empire.

The signing of this contract coincided with a visit of Prince Heinrich, the Kaiser's younger brother, to the United States. Mr. Morgan took this opportunity to invite about a hundred leading US "captains of industry" from all parts of the country to a luxurious luncheon in the honour of the German imperial guest and of the two German shipping lines. This was reciprocated by Lloyd in the following week by a reception on board its express steamer "Kronprinz Wilhelm" on its own premises in Hoboken, where 200 guests took part. These two social events marked a memorable climax in the history of American-German relations.

During those receptions Ballin made the acquaintance of Henry Edward Harriman, the then President of the Union Pacific railway company, with whom he began negotiations about Hapag's new Transpacific service from San Francisco. With the amicable agreement that was soon reached Ballin paved the way, without his anticipation, for a comprehensive cooperation between Harriman's son Averill and the group controlled by him and Dr. Wilhelm Cuno, Ballin's successor, during the early twenties, enabling Hapag the resumption of the passenger business on a large scale after the First World War.

Although Ballin had offered a 100,000 mark prize to anyone who could devise a workable cabin passenger pool, it never came about due to the complex tariff structures. When in 1908 the formation of the Atlantic Conference led to a closer cooperation between the German lines, its allied lines of the Morgan trust and Cunard, Ballin proposed as an alternative to the cabin passenger pool, the creation of a joint fund in order to scrap those older express steamers, which were no longer suitable for employment on other trade routes, and thereby avoiding that they kept the cabin prices at an artificially low level. For that purpose the five major carriers Hapag, Lloyd, Cunard, White Star and American Line, jointly accounting for about 60/70 % of the total cabin trade, were to contribute 1 £-sterl. for each passenger carried in the 1st class and 5 sh in the 2nd class. Based on the traffic statistics of 1907, it would have resulted in an annual contribution of £ 190,000 or almost 4 m marks. The records do not reveal why this farsighted approach did not find the group's approval.

Hapag and Lloyd's mail service:

Postal employees at work sorting during the voyage.

Mailbags are picked up by tender.

The passenger booking desk at the Hapag building, on 5th Avenue in New York, 1912.

Hapag and Lloyd: The two biggest shipping companies in the World (1896–1914)

When Albert Ballin joined Hapag in 1886 the company operated a mail service to New York as its trunk line and four services to the Caribbean and Mexico. Lloyd's activities had been similarly restricted to America. With the heavy fluctuations of emigration to the New World, both companies clearly recognized the commercial risks of depending too heavily on

Bremen. Verwaltungsgebäude des Norddeutschen Lloyd, Papenstrasse.

This was the magnificent administration residence of North German Lloyd at the Papen street at Bremen from 1907 to 1944. It was completely destroyed in one of the many air-raids during the war, as was the major part of the old Hanse city, together with its historic archive. There was no money available after the war for a reconstruction and the staff moved instead into the former Baggage Hall near the main station.

the passenger trade and only a few routes. As from the second half of the eighteen-eighties their services were consistently expanded worldwide.

Lloyd took the lead by inaugurating a Government-sponsored express mail service from Bremen and Antwerp to Australia and the Far East in 1886, on a monthly basis. Hapag was then still too heavily engaged in its competitive struggle against the Carr Line in the North Atlantic to be a serious competitor in these new areas, which for the first couple of years did not bring any profits for Lloyd either.

Ballin's early interest focussed on the establishment of remunerative cargo liner services so as to render his company more independent from the vicissitudes of the passenger business. His express "greyhounds" were good public relation devices to enhance Hapag's prestige, but his combined passenger-cargo liners were based in their design on high economy and thus constituted the actual "workhorses" for the purpose of making money.

The prototype of such highly economical combined passenger/cargo liners had been Hapag's P-ships, named after the first of its class, the "Pennsylvania" of 14,500 tons deadweight and a speed of 13 knots, delivered by Harland & Wolff, Belfast in 1897. It was then the largest ship in the world. Its three sister ships "Patricia", "Pretoria", and "Graf Waldersee" all designed for the Hamburg/New York trade, were built by German shipyards, their passenger capacities being: 160 in first, 180 in second class, and 2400 steerage.

Hapag's judgement that the future lay with liner cargo traffic was fully justified by the results, for almost every succeeding year brought a marked increase in the quantity of goods forwarded on its ships. Each year, a new connection, a modernized service, or an extended agency network could be recorded by both Hapag or Lloyd.

By the turn of the Century Hapag had become the largest steamship company in the world, closely followed by Lloyd which was pre-eminent in the passenger business. In 1914 both companies spanned the globe with a vast network of services, a position which due to the heavy losses in two World Wars could never again be fully recovered.

Their Annual Reports for 1913 convey impressively the size of the two companies' fleets in the last year before

the war: Hapag 190 ocean steamers, including 19 ships under construction with 1,360,000 grt; Lloyd 135 ocean vessels with 809,000 grt. In addition, both companies owned a great number of tugboats, rivercraft, motor launches and lighters, as well as extensive port facilities and real estate abroad, most of them overseas. Both companies had a total of 51,000 employees, of which 30,000 were manning their ships. In the 28 years of Ballin's management Hapag was able to pay an average dividend of 7 percent p. a. and increased its open reserves from 3.5 m to 58.9 m marks, the capital having been raised from 15 to 157 m marks. Lloyd's financial results were similarly impressive.

Between 1848 and 1913 both companies together transported a total of 17.4 million passengers, of which Lloyd carried the lion's share of 10.4 million and Hapag 7 million, both outward and homeward. Most of these passengers took their passage from Europe to the United States.

War and Devastation (1914–1919)

No other industry of a country is so adversely affected in its entire activities by a major war than ocean shipping, unless its naval forces or those of its allies effectively control the sea lanes so essential to communication. It so happened that the German shipowners, including Hapag and Lloyd, were completely caught by surprise when hostilities began in August of 1914 so that most of their ships had to take refuge in ports of neutral countries to avoid being captured by the "Entente" forces. Alone in United States ports, 64 vessels of Hapag and Lloyd found refuge. A few vessels succeeded in breaking through the blockade to return to their home ports.

Ballin had on several occasions during the preceding years used his good services to arrange political talks between leading British and German diplomats for reaching an understanding on the sensitive issue of naval armament between the two rivals. Since the German side, however, excluded him from the actual talks, they remained, much to his regret, without success. In the very last days of the "July crisis" he was once again asked by German government circles to use his good contacts to leading British

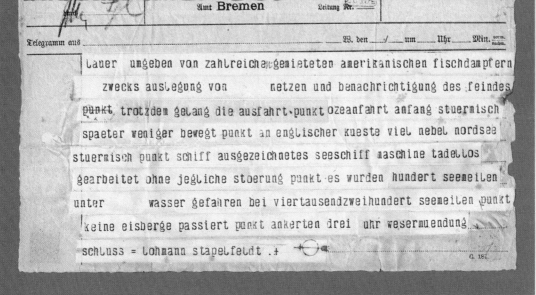

This telegram was sent by U-"Deutschland" on its first Atlantic passage on 23rd August 1916 to Bremen, reading: ...encircled by numerous chartered American fishing trawlers for the purpose of laying nets and alarming enemy stop nevertheless departure succeeded stop sailed along british coast much fog northsea stormy stop ship excellent ocean vessel engine perfectly working without any faults stop sailed one hundred miles submerged from fourthousandtwohundred nautical miles stop passed no icebergs stop anchored at three hours weser estuary ends = lohmann stapelfeldt.

U-"Deutschland" in the port of Baltimore in July 1916. The "Deutschland" accomplished two trips to the USA successfully, while its sister ship "Bremen" was lost on its first outward trip with its entire crew.

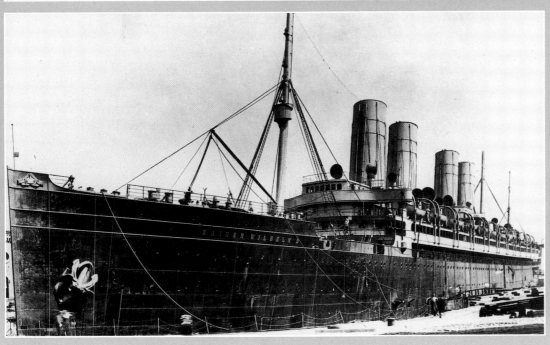

North German Lloyd's express-steamer "Kaiser Wilhelm II" Blue Ribbon winner of 1904, in dock at New York after seizure in 1917. Later she sailed again as the USS "Agamemnon".

39

The first steamer on the joint Hapag/United American Lines service — the "Mount Clay", ex Lloyd "Prinz Eitel Friedrich" — arriving at Cuxhaven on January 17, 1921.

"Bayern" leaving Hamburg in 1921.

"Albert Ballin" the first of Hapag's new North Atlantic quartette passing Cuxhaven on her maiden voyage to New York in 1923.

"Reliance" a graceful and well-known ship.

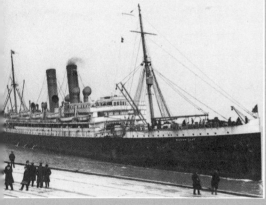

politicians in order to fathom the chances for Great Britain to stay neutral, in case of a conflict between the Continental Powers. It was a most ungratifying task, as he was neither empowered to enter negotiations on an official mission, nor was he fully briefed by his own government on the seriousness of the situation.

He later complained bitterly to a German government official "I wish that the leaders of the shipping industry had been heard, and I think it one of the greatest errors that in this most stupid of all wars, which the history of the World has ever seen, experienced businessmen were paid so little attention." For him — and this certainly applied equally to the responsible leaders of North German Lloyd — this war destroyed his life's work.

Ballin's life philosophy was directed towards international cooperation and a conciliation of interests and his broad and humane intellect therefore condemned narrow chauvinistic aspirations as counterproductive. "I am very much for peace", he wrote in October 1915 to Johannes Merck, a Hapag colleague serving with the army in Posen, "but unfortunately I must say that presently neither in the west nor in the east are there any signs for a satisfactory end to this crazy ('wahnsinnigen') war. It is as though we are living in a mad house when one reflects that these Great Powers of Europe are involved in converting Europe into a heap of ruins, all to the advantage of America and Japan."

Ballin used all his influence in the years to follow to bring this global conflict to an early end, but the military was then in command and Clausewitz's teachings that politics will always have to take top priority seemed to have been forgotten on both sides.

The moment hostilities began, the worldwide activities of both companies immediately ground to a halt. Their managements were now confronted with the serious problem of ensuring the financial survival of their huge organizations. Unlike the situation in the Second World War, when vast supply operations were conducted by the government, most of the merchant ships that had been in home waters at the outbreak, laid up idle in their ports until the armistice.

Of all the ventures started to keep up a minimum of overseas trade, the Deutsche Ozean Rhederei GmbH, set up during the war, with North German Lloyd as the majority shareholder was

perhaps the most spectacular. Its objective was the exchange of goods between Germany and the USA with cargo submarines which were literally to run under the British blockade.

One of the two submarines, the "Deutschland", under the command of the Lloyd captain Paul König successfully performed two voyages, one to Baltimore and the other to New London in the state of Connecticut in 1916, while the "Bremen" was lost on its first outbound voyage with its entire crew of 28 men.

Starting all over again (1920)

As a consequence of World War I the German Merchant Marine practically ceased to exist. All ships over 1,600 grt and half of the ships between 100 and 1,600 grt, as well as all ships under construction at the conclusion of the Versailles Peace Treaty in January 1920 were seized by the Allies. Likewise the vast property of German shipping lines abroad was totally lost. The mammoth fleets of Hapag and Lloyd had disappeared. Whatever had not already been lost by enemy action during the war was taken over by the victors.

What remained, however, were the well-established organizations of the two companies, the goodwill they enjoyed both at home and abroad and their know-how in shipping. Although the major part of their staffs had to be dismissed in the years following the outbreak of the war, a nucleus of highly trained personnel continued to work and provided the manpower basis for their recovery.

During the years 1919—20 both companies endeavoured to keep their organization afloat by concentrating on their diversified activities, such as tugboat and lighter, port and coastal services and their ferryboat passenger lines.

On the North Atlantic a somewhat curious situation had developed after the armistice that paved the way for an early recovery of Hapag and Lloyd. The US, whose pre-war activities in ocean shipping had been of little importance, had with the aid of Government subsidies established a huge merchant fleet during the war, which was further expanded by the German merchant ships, acquired by the

Peace Treaty. What was lacking on the US side, was the essential know-how of operating big shipping companies economically. In Germany the situation was exactly vice-versa. Unimpressed by a superficial hostile war propaganda, it was only too obvious for both sides then to seek to coordinate their activities by conclusion of cooperative working arrangements, so as to benefit from each other.

In 1919 Hapag had already concluded an agency contract with the US Kerr-Steamship Line for husbanding their ships in German ports. On July 4th, 1920 Ballin's successor Director General Wilhelm Cuno, with the able support of Admiral Benson, chairman of the US Shipping Board, concluded a 20 years' agreement with the American shipping magnate Averill Harriman, chairman of the United American Lines, for re-establishing the various Hapag pre-war services, except to the Far East, on a joint fifty-fifty basis while retaining both companies' corporate independence. To the Far East a similar agreement had previously been reached with the British lines of Alfred Holt & Co., Liverpool and Ellerman & Bucknall Steamship Co. Ltd., London.

This remarkable contract with the Harriman-group enabled Hapag to immediately resume its overseas activities on a large scale. North German Lloyd proceeded on a similar line. In August of 1920, an agency contract was concluded with the US Mail Steamship Company in which Lloyd took over the general agency of this company for Central Europe.

Meanwhile, several reconstruction as well as credit and financial aid contracts had been concluded by Hapag and Lloyd with the German government, enabling them to order new ships from German yards. The compensation payments which the German Reichstag had granted by the so-called "Shipping companies Recompensation Law" were diminished to such an extent by the inflation, that the German shipping companies could hardly finance one third of the number of ships originally envisaged. In addition, negotiations with the US government had begun for recompensation of the tonnage and property that had been confiscated in US ports during the war. It was to take years, however, before these came to a successful conclusion.

As of 1921, the reconstruction of the fleets of Hapag and Lloyd proceeded satisfactorily. Former German steamers were repurchased from the Allies and supplemented the newbuildings that were delivered in quick succession by German yards.

In January of 1921, the US flag-steamer "Mount Clay" (Lloyd's former Imperial mail steamer "Prinz Eitel Friedrich") opened the new Hapag/United American Lines' service from New York to Hamburg followed by the "Mount Carroll" and "Mount Clinton" in April/May.

In September of 1921, Hapag dispatched its first post-war new ship, the 8,900 ton single-screw steamer "Bayern" from Hamburg to New York with accommodation for 17 cabin and 660 third class passengers (the upgraded and more comfortably outfitted former tweendeck). "Bayern" was also the first North Atlantic passenger steamer to sail under the German flag since the war. It was followed in February of 1922 by its sister ship "Württemberg" and in March by the 16,000 ton twin-screw steamer "Hansa". The latter was, in fact, the Company's pre-war "Blue Ribbon"-winner "Deutschland". She had been in such poor shape at the conclusion of hostilities that the Armistice Commission did not consider her worth taking over. Entirely redesigned she now offered accommodation for 220 cabin and 1065 third class passengers. In February of 1922, Hapag and Lloyd were readmitted to the North Atlantic Passenger Conference.

The next important contribution to the new service were the 20,000 ton United American Lines' "Resolute" and "Reliance" starting on their maiden voyages from Hamburg and Southampton to New York in April/May of 1922. These beautiful three funnel ships had been under construction at the outbreak of war for Hapag's South American service and soon acquired great popularity among American travellers. The last unit of the U.A.L. fleet was the 17,000 ton "Cleveland" – Hapag's pre-war cruise liner of the same name – which joined the service in 1923.

Meanwhile Hapag took delivery of the first of a series of four vastly superior passenger liners from the Hamburg yard Blohm & Voss. The 20,800 ton twin-screw „Albert Ballin" with a service speed of 15.5 knots and accommodation for 250 first, 340 second, and 960 third class passengers and a crew of 415 men, started on her maiden voyage on July 4th, 1923 from Hamburg to New York.

m.v. "Milwaukee" of 16,700 grt and 16 knots, originally planned as "Carl Schurz", performed its maiden voyage from Hamburg to New York in June 1929, with a capacity of 270 first class, 290 tourist and 400 third class passengers. In 1935/36 "Milwaukee" was transformed into a cruising liner with a capacity of 560 first class passengers.

Hapag's twin-screw motor vessel "St. Louis" of 16,000 grt and 16 knots, built in 1928, and its sister ship "Milwaukee" were the first passenger liners of that size that had been equipped with diesel power, the fruits of continuous experiments and studies by Hapag's technical department since pre-war years in cooperation with the Danish East Asiatic Co. and the shipyard and motor factory Burmeister & Wain that had pioneered and developped the introduction of diesel engines in merchant shipping.

"St. Louis" served on the North Atlantic as well as for cruises for American tourists from New York into the Caribbean. In 1939 the ship under the command of Captain Gustav Schröder became famous by its transport and odyssey of 900 Jewish emigrants to Havana.

41

Hamburg=Amerika Linie

Passagier=Fahrten mit Zeppelin=Luftschiffen

Abteilung Luftschiffahrt

First **AIR CRUISE** *in History*

NEW AIR CRUISE MAP of EUROPE

A CRUISE, without precedent, challenging the interest of modern Travel America. From the windows of luxurious, giant transports of the air, you watch the fascinating panorama of Europe unfold majestically before your eyes. Official receptions all along the route. Stop-overs at important centers for sightseeing and entertainment. Special features of the trip will be attendance at the International Aeronautical

Exhibition and inspection of the celebrated airplane works of France, Holland, and Germany, besides other points of interest in England and the Continent. All expenses on land, water and air included... $1290 up. Reduced rates for aeronautic students. Inexpensive side trips by air to Ireland and Scandinavian ports.— Arrangements have been made to carry cruise passengers by plane from principal cities of the United States to the S. S. COLUMBUS.

ENGLAND
FRANCE
HOLLAND
GERMANY
SWITZERLAND
AUSTRIA

Address EXECUTIVE COMMITTEE, AMERICAN AVIATION TOUR OF EUROPE, 32 Broadway, New York City, or your local tourist agent

SEPTEMBER 8
LEAVING NEW YORK VIA FLAGSHIP COLUMBUS
RETURNING
OCTOBER 29

NORTH GERMAN LLOYD

Cruise folders free on request

Make reservations without delay

These ships indeed became highly popular among the North Atlantic travellers. In view of their advanced construction which included a passive anti-roll system that reduced rolling in heavy weather by two thirds, they were called "anti-seasick ships" by the Americans.

Next in the series to be delivered was the "Deutschland", completed in March of 1924. Due to the exhaustion ot the US immigration quota the vessel had to be laid up immediately after delivery, as she would otherwise have been sailing practically empty to New York. This was a direct result of the new US immigration law that restricted immigration by quota for the different nationalities, and led to a complete restructuring of emigrant traffic from Europe to the USA.

These new ships consolidated Hapag's position on the North Atlantic and in July of 1926, following discussion with Mr. Harriman, the passenger steamers "Reliance", "Resolute" and "Cleveland" and its liner organization were taken over from U.A.L. in return for a share of capital to the value of ten million marks. The third and fourth unit of the "Albert Ballin" class, the 21,100 ton "Hamburg" and "New York" were placed in service in 1926 and 1927 respectively enabling Hapag as from 1927 to offer a weekly service from Hamburg, Southampton and Cherbourg. In 1929—30 all four ships were fitted with new turbines and in 1933—1934 they were lengthened by 82 feet. Those alterations increased their speed to 20 knots, shortening their passage from Southampton and Cherbourg to New York from nine to seven days.

Hapag's post-war building program for the North Atlantic was completed in 1928—29 by the motor ships "St. Louis" and "Milwaukee" of 16,700 tons each, representing then the two biggest motor ships so far commissioned in the German fleet and acquired great popularity as cruising and tourist ships during the thirties.

North German Lloyd's progress since the war had been even more spectacular. Its joint service partner, the United States Mail Steamship Company, had chartered from the US Shipping Board, which had the disposition of the confiscated German ships, eleven large steamers, eight of them were former Lloyd ships: the "George Washington", "Kronprizessin Cecilie", "Kaiser Wilhelm II", "Princess Alice", "Princess Irene", "Rhein", "Neckar" and "Köln". With the exception of the "George Washington", they now sailed under new names. The two companies acted as general agents for each other on a reciprocal basis, Lloyd for Central Europe and the American company for the territory of the United States. Most important for the future was, however, the agreement that Lloyd was entitled to resume services between New York, Boston, Baltimore and Bremen with own tonnage of up to 200,000 grt.

The first ship in the new joint service calling at Bremerhaven was the US "Susquehanna" (ex "Rhein") in August 1920. The U.S. Mail S.S. Co. soon got into financial difficulties, and in September of 1921, their services were taken over by the United States Lines. This left Lloyd with a free hand to continue on its own.

In February of 1921, the 8,000 ton "Seydlitz" (built in 1903) reopened Lloyd's post-war Bremen—New York service followed at fortnightly intervals by the "Hannover" (1899) and the "York" (1906) of similar size. In 1923—24 two new ships specially designed for the New York service, the 13,000 ton "München" and "Stuttgart" were placed into service. They initially offered accommodation for 170 passengers in the 1st, 350 in the 2nd and 560 in the 3rd class with a crew of 350, and had a service speed of 15 knots. The new star in Lloyd's North Atlantic route, however, became the 32,350 ton express passenger steamer "Columbus", starting on her maiden voyage in April 1924 with a service speed of 18 knots.

The vessel had already been laid down at Danzig in 1914 for Lloyd's account and was released by the British government in compensation for a quick delivery of its earlier sister the former 34,000 ton "Columbus" to the White Star Line under the new name "Homeric". The "Columbus" was the largest ship that Lloyd had so far commissioned, offering accommodation for 480 passengers in the first, 650 in the tourist and 600 in the third class and a crew of 527. Its modern and comfortable furnishings, in combination with superb service made her one of the most popular ships on the North Atlantic route within a short time. In 1925, Lloyd completed its first rebuilding programme with the 15,300 ton "Berlin".

In 1926, Lloyd carried 46,000 westbound and 23,000 eastbound passengers in the Bremen—New York route, and with these figures regained the top rank among the Continental passenger lines.

The team of the first East-West flight from left: Major Fitzmaurice, G. von Hünefeld, Captain Köhl.

One of the most spectacular events in the history of North German Lloyd had been the first East-West crossing of the Atlantic by air on the initiative of Günther v. Hünefeld, Lloyd's corporation lawyer and head of the Public Relations department, made in 1928.
Ticker tape Parade in New York greeted the pioneer flyers in April 1928.

Arrival of the "Columbus" of 35,000 grt, on June 18, 1928 with Köhl, Fitzmaurice and von Hünefeld on board, enthusiastically welcomed by their "fans" on this side of the Atlantic.

Hapag and Lloyd also participated in the development of air transport activities at an early stage:
Hapag was general agent for German Zeppelin passages between 1910 and 1939.

North German Lloyd was offering the first Air cruises in history in Europe in combination with its transatlantic passenger service for American tourists.

North German Lloyd and Lufthansa joined forces to shorten mail transit times between Europe and North America. The new express liners "Bremen" and "Europa" provided the stimulus for this undertaking. These were each to be equipped with a catapult for boarding a seaplane that was to bring mail one day after the ship left the port of embarkation and carry it to the first port of destination a day prior to vessel's arrival. The premiere took place on July 22, 1929, when a Heinkel H 17 specially designed for this new venture took off around 450 nautical miles East of New York. It worked beautifully. On her homeward voyage the plane started even some 800 nautical miles out of Bremerhaven thereby shortcutting mail delivery by 24 hours in each direction.

The "Europa" along the Columbus quay at Bremerhaven.

The "Bremen" on her World cruise entering Pedro Miguel Locks in the Panama Canal in February 1939, by then the largest ship that had ever gone through the Canal. On both sides one can see the lorries towing the giant ocean liner through the locks.

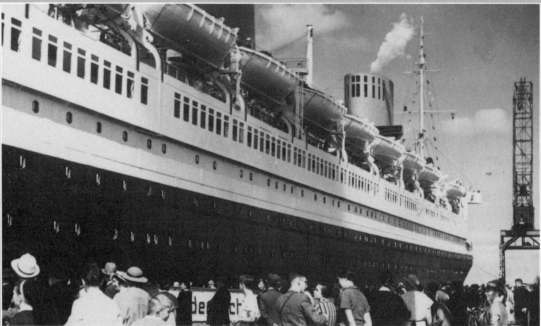

Race for the "Blue Ribbon" (1929–1939)

The good reception given to Lloyd's new passenger liners by the international travelling public encouraged the management to supplement the express service of the "Columbus" by placing orders for two new passenger liners of about 50,000 tons each and a service speed of 26.25 knots, the "Bremen" and "Europa" in Dec. 1926. They were to be delivered at the beginning of the season 1929, at a price of about 50 million marks per ship.

In 1927 Lloyd was commemorating its 70th anniversary and, due to the favourable development of world trade in general and a travelling boom in particular, Lloyd was for the first time since the war able to pay a dividend of 6 %. In addition, both Hapag and Lloyd expected the first instalments of their war indemnification by the U.S. Government after a corresponding bill had been passed by Congress, legalizing this transaction. In Bremen it was feared that Hapag, due to receive the lion's share, would immediately reinvest this new capital in passenger liners on the North Atlantic route, thereby placing it in a dominant position as competitor.

Although both ships were launched on consecutive days in August 15/16, 1928, and were christened by the German Reichspräsident von Hindenburg ("Bremen") and the US Ambassador Dr. h.c. Jacob Gould Shurman ("Europa"), the "Europa" was seriously damaged by fire while fitting out in Hamburg. The "Bremen" was therefore completed many months before her. During her maiden voyage in July of 1929, the "Bremen" was able to regain the "Blue Ribbon" for Germany after 22 years by steaming from Cherbourg to New York at an average speed of 27.8 knots with a passage of 4 days, 17 h. 42 m. Homeward she did even better with an average of 27.9 knots. The "Europa" started her belated maiden voyage in March of 1930, and even beat the westbound record of the "Bremen" slightly in spite of stormy weather. Three years later the "Europa" finally emerged as the faster of the two by improving her westbound record by 18 minutes. The "Bremen" could improve her eastbound record to 28.5 knots, however, eastbound passages do not count for the "Blue Ribbon" due to more favourable easterly winds and currents.

Lloyd's two new flag ships, the "Bremen" (51,656 grt) and the "Europa" (49,746 grt) could, with their fast transit times, have offered a weekly service from the Canal ports to New York, had they not to cover two extra sailing days per round voyage from and to Bremerhaven. Together with the "Columbus" (32,354 grt), which had been entirely refitted with single-reduction geared turbines, increasing her speed from 19 to 23 knots, a 10 days' service was offered instead from Bremerhaven calling at Southampton and Cherbourg since spring 1930. During the first year it actually achieved an average utilization of 75 % instead of the company's cautious target of 60 %.

This great success was already overshadowed, however, by the World Economic Crisis that was soon to bury all hopes of the managements of both companies.

Already in their outer appearance these new "queens" of the ocean, looked with their two squat funnels, stream-lined bridges and two masts and a raked stem, most impressive and differed considerably from any predecessor. Both ships were propelled by single-reduction geared turbines driving four screws. As the ships were constructed by two different yards, their dimensions and silhouettes differed slightly. Both had accommodations for 2,200 passengers with a crew of about 1,000 men.

Leading German architects were entrusted with the interior decoration, engaging industrial firms from all over the country for the outfitting. Even for our modern eyes, the large dining rooms and lounges, halls and cabins of all three classes captivate by their unpretentious elegance, harmony and practical comfort, breathing the fresh atmosphere of one of the leading Continental hotels of our times. The spacious swimming pool was equipped with a bar offering its guests refreshments.

In honour of the sponsor of the "Europa", US Ambassador Dr. Jacob Gould Shurman, adjacent to the ship's main dining room, there was an elegant separate dining room specially dedicated to him. Its walls were richly pannelled with rare tropical woods, partly covered with green damask. In keeping with the significance of the room, pride of place was given to two excellent paintings by Prof. E. Orlik; one a portrait of the ambassador and the other a view of Heidelberg, where Dr. Shurman had studied. These were supplemented by landscape paintings of the Neckar valley by Rudolf Sieck.

Great importance was attached to the safety installations. Apart from the most modern watertight compartments and fire-detecting and fire-fighting systems, all life-boats were equipped with watertight engines that could be operated even when the boats were fully flooded. Each lifeboat had a capacity of 145 persons so that all passengers and crew members could be easily accommodated in them. All boats could be launched simultaneously within the shortest time possible.

A catapult plane specially constructed by Heinkel for Lloyd was stationed between the two funnels. It shortened the transit time for express mail considerably, being launched about 600 up to 1,000 nautical miles from the first port of call in the US or Europe. Thus this service was a forerunner of Transatlantic airmail.

Lloyd's spectacular reappearance with its two top express steamers on the North Atlantic only seven years after its new beginning almost from scratch, had immediate repercussions on the other competitors and triggered a new race for the "Blue Ribbon".

CGT had already commissioned its 35,000 grt "Paris" in 1921, followed in 1927 by the 43,000 grt "Ile de France", and immediately felt the loss of market shares to the two German ships, whilst "Italia" reacted by ordering the two 50,000 grt express steamers "Rex" and "Conte di Savoia" on Italian yards, resulting in additional competition from Genoa. The French, therefore, ordered the 80,000 grt "Normandie" at St. Nazaire, followed by Cunard with the order for a similar ship at Newcastle, each with a speed of 30 knots.

The only crucial difference in these orders was, that, whilst all the above ships were receiving heavy subsidies, Lloyd had to finance its ships all on its own, despite repeated accusations to the contrary from abroad. It thus happened that within a few years passenger ship capacities again by far exceeded the actual demand so that profitibility quickly went overboard.

Still in 1933 the Italian liner "Rex" gained the "Blue Ribbon", only to lose it in the following years to the "Normandie" (1935), the "Queen Mary" of Cunard (1936) and USL's the "United States" (1952), which was probably the last vessel ever to hold this coveted trophy.

Rivalry of the two giants and the great depression (1927–1932)

The rebuilding of the two companies after the Great War had to be accomplished under extraordinary political and economic strains.

When the German Government passed their Fleet Reconstruction Bill, in early 1921, the total value of the amount to be repaid had been reduced by inflation to a fraction of the value of the fleets the two companies had lost through war and confiscation. Both Hapag and Lloyd, suffering from lack of own funds, had therefore to rely on their own initiatives to finance their rebuilding programs through debentures, foreign loans and repeated increases of their share capital.

Total delivery of the World's second biggest merchant fleet to the victors in combination with an annual production of 200,000 grt in newbuildings for the Allies by the German shipyards for several years to follow had pre-programmed a serious imbalance between tonnage supply and demand in world shipping by 1930.

In addition, a new US immigration law set sharply reduced immigration quotas for the different national groups, leading to a strong reduction of passenger traffic. The trade boom in the years from 1927 up to 1928, that had encouraged Hapag and Lloyd to start their follow-up rebuilding programm, turned out to be shortlived.

Economic depression and crises of enterprises and the measures taken to overcome them can, at times, be more informative than economic success, provided one takes the trouble to critically evaluate their causes and background.

Quite a few people tend, however, to consider their own experiences as being unique and therefore believe a study of past events to be a waste of time.

Hapag and Lloyd were competitors in most of their overseas liner services. Immediately prior to the outbreak of the war, serious disputes on a reallocation of their passenger quotas within the North Atlantic Conference had prompted the German Emperor to intervene and to induce the two companies to settle their grievances amicably in a comprehensive trade agreement. The war, however, prevented its implementation.

After the War the two new executive Presidents Dr. Cuno (Hapag) and privy councillor Stimming (Lloyd) soon started talks on the desirability of entering into an overall joint venture, so as to better utilize their tonnage capacities and resources and to economize on their operational costs. But the rivalries of the two Hanseatic cities Bremen and Hamburg, as well as secondary issues, time and again stood in the way of reaching an agreement.

Although Hapag, Lloyd and Hamburg-South American Line had exchanged preference shares to deter outsider domination already during the War, they still vied to outdo each other by buying up shares of other German shipping companies with the resultant mergers leading to inflated tonnage capacities and a top heavy administration.

The major banks were not innocent in these developments. The culmination came with the merger of the united fleets of the Deutsch-Austral, Kosmos- und Hugo Stinnes lines by Hapag in November of 1926, from which Hapag adopted the black, white and red funnel top, as from 1927.

The chairman of the Darmstädter and Nationalbank, one of the five leading German banks, wanted to get rid of the majority shares of these 3 companies, and was urging Hapag to acquire them, threatening to offer them otherwise to Lloyd or foreign interests. Both alternatives seemed equally alarming for Hapag, considering that they were strong competitors on several of its major liner routes. The takeover of these companies thus appeared to the Hapag board of directors as the smaller evil. The negative experiences with takeovers of the company during 1875/76 – just fifty years ago – seemed to have been forgotten. By this merger Hapag's fleet capacity became so predominant in relation to Lloyd that their talks on the Union, which was initialled with an operational agreement for the duration of 30 years in March 1926, were discontinued for almost two years. Lloyd, instead, ordered its two big express steamers "Bremen" and "Europa" together with 15 cargo liners so as to redress the balance of the market. This led to a further costly escalation of mutual competition during the next years.

In order to accomplish the merger, Hapag had to raise its stock capital in two stages by a total of 85 m Mark in the years 1926/27.

For several years, Cuno and Stimming had successfully been negotiating with the US government on the reparations for German private property confiscated in the US during the war. Among this there were 109 brand new merchant ships of totally 600,000 grt, 80 percent of which belonged to Hapag and Lloyd, as well as extensive dock facilities in several US ports.

It was most encouraging to record that the USA at an early date took exception to the vindictive behaviour of the signatories to the "Treaty of Versailles" and stuck to the principle of protecting private property as a cornerstone of its own constitution. Its "due process of law" paragraph was already incorporated into a treaty with the Kingdom of Prussia in 1785, that was extended to the German Empire as its legal successor. In 1928 Congress passed the "Settlement of War Claims Act" legalising those reparations, the values of which were fixed in June of 1930 to the total amount of 69 million dollars for Hapag and Lloyd, payable in four instalments. The two companies had agreed among each other on a share of 61 percent for Hapag and 39 percent for NGL.

In view of these reparations, already during 1925–27 Hapag and Lloyd had taken up loans with US bank consortia at favourable interest rates for financing their shipbuilding programs, partly also as a measure to assist the German shipbuilding industry, that was already then seriously suffering from unemployment.

The German government was backing these efforts by paying interest subsidies to the two companies.

In March of 1930, their increasing indebtedness and the rising pressures of the world economic crisis finally prompted Hapag and Lloyd, after several vain attempts, to join in the Hapag-Lloyd Union. This combination, though still retaining their corporate identity, had already many features of a merger. Whilst each company had its own supervisory board, the board of directors were composed of equal persons from members of both firms. The contract provided the joint operation of all services and the uniform preparation of the balance sheets with proportional sharing of profit and loss.

This "Union", however, came too late for preventing a dramatic development for the two companies shortly afterwards.

Although the agreement was established for the duration of 50 years, a period almost unbelievable in those turbulent times, rivalries between the two companies continued hardly before the ink of the agreement had dried. The new strong man in Bremen, the second Director General Ernst Glässel, was determined to counterbalance the unfavourable ratio of traffic volume for Bremen compared to Hamburg by gradual takeovers and acquisition of controlling interests in a number of shipping companies in Hamburg, Bremen and adjacent ports, although this ran counter to the letter and spirit of the agreement. The culmination came when Mr. Glässel behind the backs of the Hapag members of the board acquired and partly mortgaged a majority of 80 % of the stock of Hamburg-South America Line (Ha-Süd) to a Dutch company in exchange for a credit, guaranteeing the latter full compensation for a fluctuation of the stock price by depositing additional shares.

Moreover, Mr. Glässel acquired, likewise without prior consultation of his Hamburg colleagues, majority stocks of 90 % of the DG Neptun and of 75 % of the DDG Hansa, two prominent Bremen shipping companies, at high stock prices raising Lloyd's short term liabilities by 100 m marks. According to the Union agreement, Hapag and Lloyd had to take over 50 % of the stock capital of third companies of the other partner. These serious breaches of contract were overtaken by the escalating events, which both companies had to face in the following year.

The first two instalments of the US reparations were paid by October 1931, whereas, due to the escalating crisis, the balance of 35 million dollars was never to be forthcoming. Things took a turn for the worse. Already in November of 1930, the German government, due to its own budgetary shortfalls, prematurely reclaimed the shipbuilding credits of 50 million marks granted in 1925, which were supposed to run until 1935. Both companies, however, were unable to meet this demand as, due to the trade recession, their earnings had fallen dramatically. Further protectionist moves by many governments, including the German exchange restrictions, and import restrictions for the protection of the German agriculture accelerated the international economic crisis. Over a third of the German fleet was laid up by the end of 1931.
At the Annual General Meetings of Hapag and Lloyd in March of 1932, a loss of 30 million marks was forecast. In or-

der to avoid insolvency, shareholders were asked to provide a credit of 8 million marks each for both companies.

The big banks as major shareholders, which in the past had urged several times both Hapag and Lloyd to take over major shares of other German shipping companies that had been in difficulties, were themselves in serious trouble of liquidity due to insolvency of a number of creditors and the withdrawl of foreign deposits. They now insisted on a government guarantee for the 8 million stopgap loan. Thus, for the first time the companies had to ask their government for outright help. The government agreed to provide surety for the loan, demanding in return a cut in shares in the ratio of three to one, as well as the appointment of a trustee installed by them.

The government intervenes – German-America Line (1932–1941)

With the nomination of a trustee the direct controlling interest of the government in the conduct of affairs of both companies began.

In December 1932 a scrapping drive got underway with the assistance of the government in which 25 older vessels of Hapag and Lloyd with a total tonnage of 150,000 grt were scrapped. In February 1933 a standstill agreement was reached with the German Ministry of Finance deferring repayment of the government loans until further notice.

The seizure of power by the National Socialists, which had meanwhile taken place, also meant a rigorous turning point for the two companies. Ballin died, after thirty years of most successful activities devoted to German shipping and at the top of Hamburg-America Line, as a broken man on November 9, 1918, the day the Kaiser abdicated. One year prior to his death he had engaged the young Dr. Wilhelm Cuno, a man who accomplished an almost smooth change of leadership and who also succeeded in returning the company to the top group of world liner shipping within one decade. Cuno died on January 3, 1933, so that he was spared the humiliations of the following months. His counterpart at North German Lloyd was Privy Council Carl

Stimming, who during the years of reconstruction proved to be of a similar calibre.

On July 26, 1933, under the pressure of the new rulers, the two supervisory boards of Hamburg-America Line and North German Lloyd resigned as a body, in order to give way to new members, who were acceptable to the regime. Among those leaving their offices were men of such a high standing as the two chairman Dr. Ing. Philipp Heineken (Lloyd) and Max von Schinckel (since 1897 in Hapag's supervisory board and since 1911 in the chair), as well as Max M. Warburg, Albert Ballin's friend of many years and in Hapag's supervisory board since 1911.

Men like Max Warburg stood by both companies with help and advice as bankers in good and bad years, in case of Warburg for example with the difficult financing of the four post-war passenger liners of the "Albert Ballin"-class.

As a further step in the reorganization and financial rehabilitation of Hapag and Lloyd, upon government's insistence, shares were once again cut, this time in the proportion of five to one in the year 1934. All new shares passed into government hands, the government thus becoming the majority shareholder. The control of the enterprises, however, still rested with the board of directors, appointed by the major banks, with the government delegating its interests to the safeguard of a trustee.

The concentration of the major part of the German liner activities in the two companies had proved impracticable and from the perspective of the total economy also undesirable. Accordingly, in close consultation with the new German Government and the Cities of Bremen and Hamburg, a reapportionment of the major overseas trades was agreed on in 1935, superseding the "Union" agreement of 1930. In a new agreement the joint activities of Hapag and Lloyd were restricted to their major overseas trade areas. Traditional single services were to be operated by Hapag and Lloyd entirely autonomously. Already in 1934 the services to the East Coast of South America, to Africa and the Levant were broken up and the overseas services of those areas were transferred to the Hamburg-South America Line, the Woerman Line and the German-East-Africa Line respectively, including the tonnage under employment on those routes. Also the Intra-European services became independent again and were returned to the German lines traditionally operating on these routes. This re-allocation of trading interests was to prove its worth especially during the years of reconstruction, following the Second World War.

Objections had to be raised, however, about the manner and style with which this whole rearrangement and break up was accomplished. It had the character of a dictate, drastically ignoring the legitimate interests of the two German carriers involved. The original demand of the President of the German National Shipowners Association in his capacity as a trustee invested by the Hitler government, to completely break up Hapag and Lloyd into their single services, could only be blocked by the energetic veto of their two chairmen of the supervisory boards Emil Helfferich (Hapag) and Karl Lindemann (Lloyd) and by their patient negotiations with the government.

As an essential step for the improvement of the effectiveness of the two head offices, a far reaching decentralisation of the management responsibilities from the Board of directors to the route managers was decided on.

For that purpose the lines' managers obtained for their divisional responsibilities the competence and duties of managing directors of a limited liability company and accounting was also to take place separately for each service according to the regulations of a limited liability company.

It was further stated: The line's manager acts for the daily business and for matters concerning his liner service independently and determines the organisation of the division under his command. Within the scope of his competence granted he takes the full responsibility for his liner service. He also participates, also if not being a member of the board, at the meetings of the board of directors.

It was thus only consistent that he was also free to cover the supply of services from the free market, should the services and supplies offered by the affiliated companies of the own enterprise not prove competitive.

Hapag's annual report of 1935 amplifies on this as follows: "We have been guided by the aspiration, to give the experiences of the shipping business of our leading employees stronger effect and to obtain a closer cooperation between shore and ship. We hope that these measures will render business

activities simpler and more flexible and that it will ensure an utmost economy within the company, most of all that it will increase the sense of responsibility and the pleasure in one's work for each employed in the firm to a maximum extent."

By the end of 1938 Hapag, after its reorganisation had been completed, had again reached the top position in German shipping with 100 ocean vessels totalling 715,000 grt and about 13,000 employees. Also North German Lloyd could consolidate its position with 70 ocean vessels and 566,000 grt, including the sail training ship "Kommodore Johnson", a four-masted barque.

In September 1941, with retroactive effect from January 1 of the same year, the government remitted all shipping shares in its possession to private interests, so that from that year onwards, the two companies stood once again on their own feet.

The North Atlantic trade, however, that had yielded permanent operational losses since 1932, was reorganized in a separate entity under the trade name "German America-Line Incorp.", in which Hapag and Lloyd had shares of 25 percent each, with the German government holding the balance of 50 %. The North Atlantic express liners of Hapag and Lloyd were transferred to the new company and Hapag was relieved of its financial liabilities for the new passenger liner "Vaterland" (35,000 grt, 24 knots) then under construction at Blohm & Voss. This newbuilding was destroyed by an air-raid at the end of the war.

Once more Hapag was endangered by the new majority shareholder Philipp Reemtsma, when he demanded from the chairman of the supervisory board, Emil Helfferich, the conversion of the stock corporation into a partnership, which Helfferich strictly rejected.

When Helfferich, in the course of the negotiations, felt let down in this question even by his own board of directors, he resigned in October 1941. Like a miracle, Hamburg-America Line remained, however, a stock corporation.

For Reemtsma, in the first place taxation deliberations may have come into play. Nevertheless, some of his beliefs in favour of a partnership still deserve our attention today. For example, he questioned the wisdom of a shipping company, which has to face severe worldwide competition, having

to disclose its own financial affairs, due to its statutory publication obligations, since by doing so it will automatically be placed at a disadvantage viz-a-viz competitors with a partnership structure.

Total destruction — for the second time (1939—1945)

The start of the Second World War in September of 1939, immediately put an end to all German liner operations. Ships in transit at the outbreak of the war were interned in neutral ports or tried to reach home waters. The best remembered feat is, perhaps, the dash of the "Bremen" from New York, past enemy patrols to Murmansk in the Soviet Union and thence, a few months later, to Bremerhaven.

Many modern freighters proved their worth as auxiliary cruisers and blockade runners bringing, against immense odds, vital raw materials, such as rubber, tin and tungsten from the Far East. Other ships were used for the extensive troop convoy and supply operations, carried out in the European war theatre. The surviving German merchant ships of about 2.1 million grt — among them several Hapag and Lloyd passenger liners — helped in January up to May 1945 in the greatest refugee transport ever, evacuating two million refugees and wounded soldiers threatened by the advance of the Red Army, bringing them across the Baltic to safety in the Western parts of the disintegrating German territory.

Out of the total German fleet of about 4.5 m grt at the outbreak of the war, 3 m grt were lost as a result of enemy action. About 3,000 sailors lost their lives aboard their ships. On May 9, 1945, the day of capitulation, the tonnage of the German merchant fleet had dwindled by 66 % to 1.5 m grt, but was still sufficient to relieve the catastrophic food situation in Germany by the transport of vital goods.

The Potsdam Treaty of August 1945 decreed, however, that the remaining German merchant ships, were to be delivered to the UdSSR, the UK and the United States. 34 of those ships were, upon the Allies' instructions, loaded with gas ammunition and sunk in the North Sea, were they still rest today.

This was a break of promise given by General Dwight D. Eisenhower in two

The piers on the West side of Manhattan, N.Y.: the great days of the passenger liners (1939); top to bottom: "Conte di Savoia" (Italia), "Aquitania" (Cunard), "Britannic" (Cunard), "Normandie" (CGT), "De Grasse" (CGT), "Columbus" (Lloyd), "Bremen" (Lloyd), "Hamburg" (Hapag).

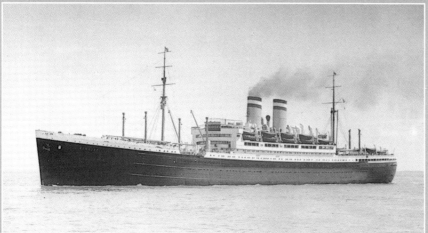

The "Hamburg" (2) (22,117 grt) after having been jumboised in 1933/34 increasing her speed by 2 knots to 20 knots so as to better compete with Lloyd's new "Blue Ribbon" winners "Bremen" and "Europa". Sister ship "New York" (Hapag) received the same new look, completing the modernisation program of the "Albert Ballin" quartet.

This was the silhouette of Hapag's new trans-Atlantic liner "Vaterland" (II) of 35,000 grt which was to replace the quartet of the "Albert Ballin" class during the "forties", but was never completed due to the outbreak of World War II.

After the last shipbuilding and shipping restrictions had been lifted by the Allies in 1952, Hapag and Lloyd went to work to rebuild their pre-war services, most of them in the form of joint services, as in case of the North Atlantic, the US-Gulf/South Atlantic and the US/Canada North Pacific services. Among the first ships entering their post-war services were:

Lloyd's "Bieberstein" of 8,325 dwt and 16.5 knots passing under the Lions Gate Bridge, Vancouver.

Hapag's cargo liner and training ship "Heidelberg" of 11,480 dwt and 16.5 knots.

Hapag's "Hamburg" of 4,460 dwt and 12 knots.

BBC broadcasts to the German sailors on April 18 and 19, 1945, when he appealed to them not to scuttle their ships, since every German vessel would be urgently needed to maintain the important sea trade and to transport supplies. Wages would continue to be paid, working conditions to be maintained and social insurances to remain in force.

Post-war restrictions and impeded recovery (1945–1952)

The situation, with which the German private shipping companies had been confronted at the end of the Second World War, is best reflected in Hapag's Annual Report for 1947, dated June, 1948:

"On May 27, 1947 our company was able to look back at its centennial. We have commemorated this day quietly. For the second time in its history this shipping company has lost its total fleet through war. The life's work of generations has been destroyed. Under these circumstances there was no inducement for celebrations.

We may, however, look back at this Century during which our company for decades took a leading position in the world, with pride, and to remember with gratitude all those who have dedicated their life's work to this firm ...

For decades of laborious and sometimes loss involving pioneer work our company in conjunction with those shipping companies, with which we later merged, the Deutsch-Australische Dampfschiffs-Gesellschaft AG and Deutsche Dampfschiffahrtsgesellschaft Kosmos AG, had established shipping lines, which connected Germany with almost all parts of the world and not only promoted the development of German foreign trade, but also contributed its share to promote trade and welfare of the neighbouring European countries and of the partners overseas. Those shipping companies have enabled the large stream of people, which in the course of those decades looked for a new homeland overseas, a safe and reliable passage. During that time span our company has contributed essentially to progress in shipping and its technology.

The confidence that has been extended to our shipping company by a great number of passengers and shippers of all nations for a century reaf-

firms us in our belief that our endeavours have been channelled in the right direction to serve the welfare of all people in peaceful competition. We therefore also consider it our future task to carry on in the tradition of the founders of our shipping company.

Due to the regulations imposed by the Occupying Powers, German ships are still prohibited from moving overseas. For this reason a resumption of our business overseas was not possible during the year under review either. We have, however, endeavoured, within the scope of the possibilities after Germany's collapse, to obtain revenues by employment of our working funds in other activities.

In cooperation with charitable organizations in Germany, we have arranged the dispatch and distribution of care parcels from abroad. During the course of 1947 it was possible to successfully further develop this department by reviving foreign contacts."

With the total loss of the pre-war fleets, and in view of the severe restrictions, that were in force for German shipowners in the first years after the war, Hapag and Lloyd had for the second time within 30 years to dismiss most of their manpower; Hapag's staff had dwindled from 14,000 employees in 1939, including 8,600 sailors, to 79 in 1947.

With a relaxation of the shipping and shipbuilding restrictions as from 1950 – the last regulations were dropped in April, 1951 – both companies agreed to continue with their pre-war cooperation as the only way to resume their traditional liner services overseas to a moderate degree, in step with the development of West Germany's overseas foreign trade.

This time the situation was much more desolate than in 1918. The newly elected Federal German Government was confronted with such a staggering task of rebuilding the country, that it was only able to assist its shipowners with small credits at low interest rates and certain tax relaxations. In this context, the Marshall Plan Aid and its ERP funds provided a valuable complementary measure to enable German shipowners, as from 1950, to acquire secondhand ships on a moderate scale and to place their first orders for new oceangoing vessels. Thus German shipowners were again called upon to look for themselves for financing the greater part of their reconstruction program, by way of borrowings and a gradual raising of their stock capital.

Fast cargo liner services to all US coasts and the Great Lakes (1953–1967)

In 1950/51 only, after an interruption of 11 years, Hapag and Lloyd were in a position to resume their North Atlantic services jointly, initially with charter tonnage, later with own ships.

Apart from New York, Philadelphia, Baltimore and Norfolk/New Port News were regularly served. Little by little additional ports were included in the schedule and the tonnage increased. Thus the service could be improved to weekly sailings as from March 1953. Now as before great importance was attributed to this trade route and service.

But it also remained, now as in the past, a highly contested market with numerous competitors.

Hapag resumed its overseas activities with the reopening of its West Indies/Central America East Coast service in April 1950, having initially started it in 1871.

Between 1950 and 1953 joint services were inaugurated to Cuba, Mexico and US Gulf ports, West Coast Central and South America and to the Far East.

The year 1954 will be remembered as a milestone in both Companies' histories, as four additional services were inaugurated:

In February Hapag resumed its Indonesia service jointly with N.S.M. Oceaan, an affiliated Dutch company of the Blue Funnel line.

In April Hapag and Lloyd dispatched their first vessel in a new joint service together with Ahrenkiel & Bene and the Hamburg-Chicago Line to Canada (Atlantic) and the Great Lakes. A weekly service was offered from Antwerp, Rotterdam, Bremen, Hamburg and vice versa to and from Quebec, Montreal, Toronto, Cleveland, Detroit, Milwaukee, Chicago, Sarnia and Hamilton.

During the first three years charter tonnage had to be employed, and as of 1958 new own ships of the "Weissenburg" and "Naumburg"-class of 4,650 dwt capacity and 14 knots ser-vice speed, with passenger accommodation for 12 passengers in the cabin-class entered the service. They had a crew of 37 men and were excellent ships.

Already one year later, in 1955, the frequency of sailings could be doubled to twice-weekly.

June 1954 saw, after an interruption of 15 years, the reopening of Hapag and Lloyd's Europe-West Coast of North America joint service.

In July 1954, after commissioning of modern turbine express liner ships of about 10,000 tons carrying capacity, the TS "Weserstein" (Lloyd) was despatched, as the first post-war ship, from the Continent to Australia and inaugurated a new Hapag-Lloyd joint service with sailings every four weeks.

In the new services both companies had to use secondhand or converted tonnage in the beginning, such as the 13,000 dwt "Nabob", a former Canadian escort carrier (CVE 77), which in 1951 was Germany's largest ship. As from 1950, new ships began to join their fleets, among them six motor ships of the "Rheinstein"-class of about 5,000 t carrying capacity were ordered by Lloyd from Bremer Vulkan. They were employed in the North Atlantic and in the US-Gulf/South Atlantic services.

In steps with expanding trade, larger and faster ships, such as the four "Tübingen"-class vessels of 8,500 dwt and 17 knots providing accommodation for 12 passengers, replaced them as from 1955.

These vessels, fast and seaworthy ships, were equipped with a variety of advanced cargo gear including reefer and tank space, allowing them to trade nearly everywhere and also to cater for the growing trend towards heavier unit-loads. Some of these ships, that were sold 1970 or later, can still be seen trading today under other flags.

Fortnightly services were offered at first on such routes as to the US Gulf or the US West Coast. Increasing trade volumes soon allowed weekly sailings, however.

On April 1, 1959, with the opening of the St. Lawrence Seaway, a new joint service of Hapag, Lloyd and Ernst Russ as a new partner, was started with larger tonnage to Canada and the Great Lakes. During the summer a weekly express cargo and passenger service was offered to the range of ports mentioned earlier, while during the winter, due to ice barriers, the service had to be reduced to fortnightly sailings to the St. Lawrence river ports only. The service was continued and even extended up to 1975, when containerisation drew more and more cargo via the US Atlantic ports, causing its abandonment after the close of the season in that year.

When Hapag-Lloyd commemorated the centennial of its service between Europe and the US Gulf on October 1, 1967, they were offering an average of five sailings per month from US Gulf ports to the Continent, crossing the Atlantic in 10 days. Modern multi-purpose ships of the "Hanau/Hattingen"-class of 8,900 dwt and a speed of 17.5 knots provided the backbone of this service.

Passenger Shipping Resumed – The fifth "Bremen" (1954–1971)

Following World War II the difficulties of starting practically from scratch were coupled with uncertainty about which direction shipping would take. Both Hapag and Lloyd were initially preoccupied with the build-up of cargo fleets, but soon there were thoughts of expanding into the passenger sector.

Hapag remained conservative in this sector. In December 1951 Hapag became the husbanding agent for the Home Lines and Greek Lines, both headquartered in New York, for their passenger liners "Italia", 16,700 grt, and "Homeland", 11,000 grt, which jointly traded as Mediterranean Lines Inc., Panama, after the Hapag-Lloyd travel Bureau Inc., jointly operated by Hapag and Lloyd, had become the general agents for their North Atlantic services. This enabled the travel bureaus for the first time after the war to again offer ships passages, for emigrants in particular, on a larger scale.

Hapag's husbanding agreement for the "Italia" was prolonged for a further 5 years in 1957. In 1958 Hapag became general agent for the "Hanseatic", 30,000 grt, of the newly founded Hamburg-Atlantic Line and was entrusted with the husbanding of the ship. Hapag provided the ship's com-

The fifth "Bremen" on her maiden voyage in 1959.

An elegant, fast vessel of 32,000 grt with a speed of 23 knots, she was specially refurbished from stem to stern for the transatlantic passenger route, on which she faithfully served for 12 years. During the winter months the "Bremen" sailed from New York on leisure cruises to the Caribbean. These cruises were very popular with American passengers, and many of them made at least one cruise on the "Bremen" each year.

mand and the crew. The contract remained in force until 1966, when the "Hanseatic" was almost completely destroyed by fire on the pierside in New York and was later sold for scrapping in Hamburg.

In 1957 Hapag acquired the Swedish passenger liner "Patricia" and after reconstruction commissioned her under the name "Ariadne" of 7,800 grt for pleasure cruising. She soon proved, however, too small and consequently unremunerative and was sold after a few years. She was nonetheless a beautiful and popular ship.

Developments with North German Lloyd took a different direction. In Bremen one was determined to mobilize again the company's comprehensive know-how and its excellent international standing for a third time and decided to reactivate its passenger business early 1954.

With the mv "Gripsholm", later renamed the "Berlin", Lloyd resumed its passenger service after an interruption of fifteen years. The very popular "Berlin" proved a fortunate decision, especially in transporting a new wave of emigrants, and Lloyd, encouraged by its success, soon decided to put a second passenger ship in service.

Purchasing the laid-up French transatlantic liner mv "Pasteur", Lloyd extensively remodelled and modernized and eventually renamed this additional passenger ship "Bremen". The new "Bremen", latest in a series of five Lloyd ships with that prominent name, was put into service according to plan in 1959 amidst much public attention on both sides of the Atlantic. This new highlight in Lloyd's history came in the belief that, despite rapidly increasing air traffic, sufficient passenger business for a medium-sized German flag ship was still to be found on the Atlantic.

In 1965, Lloyd acquired a third passenger ship the Swedish "Kungsholm", to be renamed "Europa".

Both Hapag and Lloyd also resumed their pre-war passenger service to the Far East employing new combined passenger-cargo vessels with a cabin capacity for 86 first class passengers. The Transatlantic passengers service was continued until 1971.

In the 125 years of their regular passenger services Hapag and Lloyd carried a total of 25 million passengers worldwide, of whom the greater part had travelled to and from the United States.

A poster of North German Lloyd's post-war passenger service reflecting tradition and progress with its trio "Bremen", "Europa" and "Berlin", symbolic names for thousands of European and American travellers across the Atlantic.

The new mv "Europa": Highest standards in worldwide cruising (1982)

The great popularity of the "Europa" as a cruise vessel in the seventies encouraged Hapag-Lloyd to order a new vessel in 1978 that was to be presented to a fastidious travelling public equipped with the latest developments in technology and design. The new "Europa" embarked upon her maiden voyage in January 1982 rounding the coasts of Africa. She is the largest and also still the newest cruise vessel sailing under the German flag. This ship and her crew also soon gained great popularity among her passengers.

In 1983 the ship already embarked on a world cruise lasting 115 days. The voyage comprised several segments, so as to give passengers more flexibility in selecting their favourite route. Timing was planned in such detail that the ship arrived during the peak season in the respective region. Thus, for instance, passengers experienced the famous cherry-blossom season whilst in Japan. MV "Europa" was during that voyage also a prominent guest of the tricentennial celebrations of the beginnings of German emigration to both coasts of the USA.

Meanwhile this ship has travelled to all continents of the globe, calling also at the exotic islands in the South Sea.

The program of the "Europa" also extends to the popular Northland voyages as well as to cruises to the Baltic and the Mediterranean. The planners of the voyages do not only direct their attention to interesting ports and routes, but arrange for especially attractive land excursions as for instance from Shanghai to Peking in April 1989.

Everything on board the "Europa" focusses on the recreation and comfort of the passengers. Twelve decks provide generous space, with the living quarters in the quiet front section and public rooms for a variety of leisure activities at the rear. Unique cabin sizes (each double-bed cabin is 226 sq. ft.) and design are a few of the ways through which Hapag-Lloyd continues to offer the highest standards in cruising. With its accommodation for 600 single class passengers, this ship has an unusually favourable ratio between size (33,800 grt) and passen-

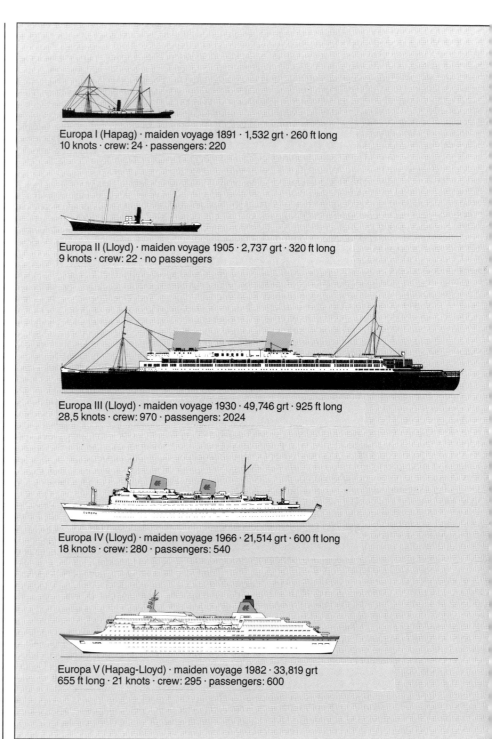

Europa I (Hapag) · maiden voyage 1891 · 1,532 grt · 260 ft long
10 knots · crew: 24 · passengers: 220

Europa II (Lloyd) · maiden voyage 1905 · 2,737 grt · 320 ft long
9 knots · crew: 22 · no passengers

Europa III (Lloyd) · maiden voyage 1930 · 49,746 grt · 925 ft long
28,5 knots · crew: 970 · passengers: 2024

Europa IV (Lloyd) · maiden voyage 1966 · 21,514 grt · 600 ft long
18 knots · crew: 280 · passengers: 540

Europa V (Hapag-Lloyd) · maiden voyage 1982 · 33,819 grt
655 ft long · 21 knots · crew: 295 · passengers: 600

Hapag-Lloyd's flag ship and Queen of the oceans the 33,819 grt „Europa" (5) placed into service January 1982 raising worldwide cruising for sea tourists to new standards, ever since these pleasure trips were first introduced by Hapag and Lloyd in 1890/91. "Europa" was one of the prominent Tricentennial guests of the American-German celebrations when calling at New York for the first time on October 5th, 1983, on her combined US-Atlantic-Caribbean cuise.

MV "Europa" '90

Club Belvedère

Restaurant on the main deck

Fancy-dress ball

Lido pool

Double-cabin (21 m^2)

Delfter tavern

ger space (56,3 grt per passenger). Shipping for pure pleasure was first performed by the excursion trips of the Hamburg-America Line and the North German Lloyd in the years 1890–91. Today ocean shipping for the purpose of recreation has reached new dimensions. They are being realised in the cruising programs of the "Europa" which change every year. After its reconstruction in December 1989 mv "Europa" finally advanced to the top rank of the international cruising fleet. Since the Christmas-/ New Years voyage 1989/90 all passengers can enjoy their meals jointly during a single sitting. This was so to speak a jubilee present from the shipping company to the centennial of the beginning of cruising for all its passengers.

MV "Europa" is the result of 100 years experience in the cruising business: a floating luxury hotel which offers security, high living comfort, lucullian palate pleasures and a rich selection of recreative facilities and cultivated entertainment. An attentive crew takes care for your well-being at sea as well as during land excursions thereby enabling you to discover the world for once from the fascinating ship's perspective.

Containers replace Passengers in transatlantic Shipping (1968–1988)

When Sea-Land's "Fairland" arrived with a full load of 35 ft. containers in Bremen from New York in May of 1966, its initiator Malcom McLean had triggered a revolution in ocean transport which in its significance can only be compared with the change from sail to steam one hundred years earlier.

Hapag's and Lloyd's management, although at first sceptical, soon began to realize that his new concept, when organized in the proper way, could not only reduce the escalating cargo handling costs in ports, but also offer enormous savings for users and operators in the overall transport chain.

In joint consultations between Hamburg and Bremen it was decided that in view of the considerable capital investments involved, this new concept should be realized as a joint venture between the two old rivals in order not to repeat the costly experience of the late twenties.

In November 1967, therefore, the two companies set up the Hapag-Lloyd Container Lines by combining their North Atlantic services, and each ordered from German ship yards two cellular containerships of 14,000 grt, with a capacity of 736 TEU and a service speed of 19 knots. As supporting measures, the companies re-organized and merged their inland sales offices and set up the German Container Service (DCD), with the task of controlling container positioning and coordinating inward and outward movements.

It could already be foreseen at this point that other trades, too, would soon follow in containerization.

Between October 1968 and March 1969, the first four Hapag-Lloyd containerships, "Weser Express" (Lloyd), "Elbe Express" (Hapag), "Mosel Express" (Lloyd), and „Alster Express" (Hapag) entered the North Atlantic service. They had the distinction of being the first purpose-built full containerships in the world.

These ships, which replaced a greater number of conventional vessels on the North Atlantic, inaugurated a weekly full container service between Europe and the North American East Coast.

Hapag-Lloyd never adhered to the "one-port" theory, so frequently put forward in the container transport business. On the contrary, they were constantly at pains to offer an equally good service to as large a group of clients as possible and to improve the range still further. This was reflected primarily in the gradual extension of the service to further European and US-ports, by means of either direct or feeder services, as well as by the later extension of the full container service to Canada.

The vessels were equipped with stabilizers and bow-thrusters. The stabilizers sharply reduced rolling during heavy weather so as to avoid damage, whilst the bow-thrusters greatly improved vessel's manoeuverability in ports and locks, so that in case of need they could also berth and unberth without tug assistance.

Other European lines regularly serving the North Atlantic took the step towards containerization by forming consortia, such as ACL and DART.

The next areas to be containerized were the trade routes between Europe and Australia and the Far East. As the greater distances required much larger vessels, it also increased proportionately the capital investment and the resultant commercial risk.

The old established lines on these routes therefore considered it necessary to cooperate in completely novel combinations such as ANZECS, TRIO and SCANDUTCH. These joint ventures, although reducing the individual companies' autonomy and operational independence, were considered essential by the participants in order to achieve a maximum capacity utilization of their tonnage through so-called slot-charter agreements whilst also offering their clients a great number of advantages such as high frequency of sailings, a reliable and high quality service, a reduction in pilferage and cargo damage, and, above all, a marked lowering of overall transport costs.

During the seventies more and more shippers took full advantage of the economies of the containers, all the more so as Hapag-Lloyd and some of its competitors showed a great flexibility in accommodating all varieties of liner cargo aboard their ships, that seemed at first sight unsuitable for transportation in those boxes. Apart from the standard 20 ft. and 40 ft. containers, shippers are offered a great variety of other types such as "open tops", "flats", "platforms", "insulated", "reefer", "ventilated" and "tank" containers (see also table on p. 73). In order to guarantee safe transport, all containers are constantly subjected to checks by the company's own experts.

The increased volume of traffic made a "jumboization" of the four "Weser Express"-class vessels from 736 to 1,100 TEU necessary. This was carried out during the winter 1973–74. Within short these dimensions again could not satisfy demand so that the second generation of ships with a capacity of 1,750 TEU and a speed of 21.5 knots were ordered for delivery between October 1977 and July 1978, and were commissioned in the following order: "Stuttgart Express", "Düsseldorf Express", Nürnberg Express", and "Köln Express" of 32,470 tdw each. They sailed each Thursday from Hamburg and on further fixed week days from other Continental ports and from Greenock to Halifax and U.S. Atlantic ports.

CMS "Elbe Express" (1100 TEU) passing the Golden Gate Bridge at San Francisco in her second "career" as Trans-pacific Service.

The beginnings of ocean container services: "Elbe Express" at the new con-tainer terminal in Hamburg.

The "Stuttgart Express" — one of the four new North Atlantic second generation container ships of 1,750 TEU each — welcomed on her maiden voyage in the port of New York in October 1977.

In the January/February 1983 edition of Lloyd's of London's periodical "Export Shipping" it was stated:

"In terms of reliability, Hapag-Lloyd's efficiency was outstanding even in a market where high quality is the order of the day. The German carriers kept an average of 0.17 days off schedule during the period under review. – The best rating so far uncovered by Lloyd's Export Shipping."

In the **US-Gulf/South Atlantic** another fascinating and revolutionary unit load concept, the "Lighter aboard Ship" (LASH) Service, was started jointly in 1972 by Hapag-Lloyd and Holland-Amerika Lijn, Rotterdam, under the trade name "Combi Line" with the two sister ships "Bilderdijk" (HAL) and "München" (H-L), of 44,600 tdw each, built by Cockerill, Antwerp, with a carrying capacity of 83 barges each of 388 t. The ships were equipped with a gantry crane for handling the lighters, so that they could be loaded/discharged independently anywhere in the large ports in a couple of hours in the estuaries of the Mississippi, Missouri, Schelde, Rhine and Weser respectively. The barges were manoeuvered up to 13 at a time by special tugboats all the way to their final destinations e. g. in Chicago or the Ruhr area. The westbound cargo consisted mainly of iron and steel, but also of heavy and oversize pieces including total industrial plants, which were loaded at suppliers' premises and delivered to the receiver's door step. Forest and agricultural products apart from general cargo were carried eastbound.

The system worked extremely well and economically for all parties, as long as sufficient cargo was available and the freight rates obtainable from the major shippers remained adequate.

The tragic loss of the "München" on her 62nd voyage in a heavy storm in mid-Atlantic on December 13, 1978 led to the abandonment of this service one year later.

Apart from the LASH service, containerization also commenced in 1974 in the US-Gulf/South Atlantic with the employment of the semi-container vessels "Ludwigshafen", "Leverkusen", "Hoechst" and "Erlangen" of 16,265 tdw and 23 knots. These were converted in 1978/79 into full container ships of 950 TEU each.

Hapag-Lloyd today offers a weekly full container service jointly with ACL and CGM from Continental Europe and U.K. to Savannah, Miami, Houston, New Orleans and Mobile and vice-versa with five ships of between 1500/2290 TEU.

Also in the **North Pacific** trade to and from the USA/Canada containerization took place in steps. Hapag-Lloyd has served this trade route for 90 years and it is thus by far the oldest European liner service in that area. In 1971 the Euro-Pacific service, a joint venture between Hapag-Lloyd, CGT and Holland-America Line was established offering a weekly semi-container service. Since the end of 1978 modern full container ships of 1,450 TEU and 19 knots speed of the "America Express"- and "Alemania Express"-class were employed in a combined service with the West Coast of Central America. Our partners remained the same but just changed their names as a result of mergers etc. into CGM and Incotrans.

Due to the completely different trade structures both services were again served separately as of November 1984.

Between 1985 and 1988 Johnson Scan Star joined the group as the major North Pacific carrier by way of a slot-charter agreement. After its withdrawal from this consortium in 1988 Hapag-Lloyd took over the largest part of its tonnage and thereby doubled its ship capacity from two to four container ships and is since then the biggest shareholder in this weekly service. In the same year TFL and Sea-Land also concluded slot-charter agreements with the North Pacific-service without, however, participating with own tonnage in this trade.

The USA ocean trade with the exception of the US-Gulf is still characterized by a considerable imbalance in favour of the European export. As a result, ships in the westbound direction are generally much better utilized than on their eastbound leg, so that eastbound they frequently have to sail with empty space and empty containers. The American export to Europe consists mostly of agricultural and forest products including reefer cargo from the West Coast, whilst mainly finished products from the food sector, machinery, chemicals and automobiles are carried from Europe.

Since January 1978 the four container ships of the "Weser Express"-class were transferred from the North Atlantic to the West Coast for the re-opening of the **Transpacific** service. This, due to its enormous foreign trade volume, far and away most important area in world seatrade also belonged to Hapag-Lloyd's traditional pre-war services, which had to be discontinued during and between the two world wars and the ensuing worldwide economic turbulences. It was therefore only a logical step of the shipping company to close this last gap in its global container services at the appropriate time.

With the establishment of the Transpacific service Hapag-Lloyd again entered after several decades into a trade which did not serve any European ports.

The Transpacific is, however, not only the most important world seatrade economically but due to its long ocean distances, its enormous geographic diversity and its peculiar competitive restraints by the U.S. liner shipping regulations, also became one of the most difficult and challenging regions operationally. The successful implementation of such a container service, therefore, requires most careful preplanning with regard to its logistics, manpower and tonnage supply as well as adequate financial staying power.

Very soon it became clear that the timing of the resumption of this liner service was ill-chosen and that the tonnage employed was too small to run a profitable service on a longterm basis. All further steps towards an improvement of the service quality – which could be up-graded through the addition of two further container ships to weekly sailings as of 1979 and also by a slot-charter and sailing agreement that was concluded with Sea-Land Services Inc. in 1984 – proved to be inadequate due to the enormous over-tonnaging in the market and the resultant drastic decline of ocean freight rates.

Therefore, Hapag-Lloyd decided to suspend its only cross-trade – which is a service exclusively between foreign ports – from the end of 1985 until further notice. The special conditions of the American market and the highest growth rates of the Transpacific in world seatrade comparison would make it advisable for a shipping company of the standard of Hapag-Lloyd, however, to dedicate special attention to this seatrade also in future.

The company still belongs to the leading container operators in the world today and carried a total of 7 million TEU (20'-container-units) in its first twenty years of worldwide container services by the end of 1988.

Rescuing of human life at sea — an unwritten law

The history of the North America services would remain incomplete if only the technical and organisational performance was reported upon and if tribute was not also paid to the men and, above all, the seamen who in the course of five generations have manned our ships and have brought the passengers and the highly valuable general merchandise that have been entrusted to them safely and punctually to their ports of destination. The great importance attached by the responsible men of both companies from the start to a careful selection and extensive training of their permanent staff of employees on board and ashore, has already been mentioned at the beginning. Irrespective of all technical achievements, especially in the service industry sector, the human being remains by far the most important capital of a business enterprise and requires for its full mobilisation leadership and solicitude.

Particularly in emergency situations and at times of extreme physical and mental stress a team, be it on board or ashore, but also each individual must stand the test, and the fortunate outcome of an undertaking, in which not seldom human life is at stake, frequently depends upon personal initiative and strength of character.

Only two cases will be quoted below in the sober language of the radio traffic between ship's command and the head offices in Bremen and Hamburg respectively from the long record of rescue operations, in which ships of both companies were involved and which received international high praise and acknowledgement.

On 15.3.1886 North German Lloyd received from its general agency in New York the following telegram:

"Oregon" sunk by collision with a schooner between Shinnecock and Fire Island. "Fulda" took from board of "Oregon" 180 cabin, 66 intermediate, 389 tween deck passengers as well as 255 crew members. They were landed here yesterday noon and were taken care of on board until this morning. The arrival of "Fulda" was delayed by 16 hours. What cost recovery shall we demand?"

Express steamer "Fulda" (Lloyd) 5,125 grt, built 1883, 16 knots, rescued 896 castaways of the Cunard-steamer "Oregon" on 14.3.1886

North German Lloyd replied in English as follows:

"Highly gratified having been instrumental in saving so many lives. No claim."

This incident caused at that time much attention in Europe as well as in America, as the "Oregon" — only in operation for a few years — was considered one of the most modern and fastest steamers of the British Cunard Company. All people on board the ship were rescued. The "Oregon" sank in the same night. All 896 castaways could be landed on the following morning by "Fulda" in New York. The ship sailed under the command of Captain Ringk.

On 19.12.1934 Norddeichradio received the following radio message from Commodore Kruse of the Hapag-steamer "New York":

"New York" received Tuesday from "Sisto" request for salvage, steamed back at WNW-gale, force nine, tremendous sea, reached "Sisto" 18.00 hours, where tanker "Mobiloil" assisted without success for 24 hours. Salvage due to weather situation presently impossible, remained near "Sisto", successively arrived "Aurania", "Europa", "Gerolstein" and other ships; agreed upon salvage work with "Aurania". 22.30 hours "Sisto" requested rescueing crew owing to threatening situation of vessel. "Aurania" was requested to pump oil weather-side of wreck. "Europa" illuminated the wreck with search light. "New York" steamed leeward, hoisted out lifeboat with Second Officer Wiesen, 10 sailors. After two hours of extraordinary hard work under tremendous swell rescue work successfully accomplished. Wreck crew had to jump individually over-board and was fished out by lifeboat. Wednesday 2.00 hours total wreck crew 16 men completely and uninjured on board. Voyage continued, wreck still drifting, danger for shipping. — Kruse."

Boat drill on board the Hapag-passenger steamer "Milwaukee" (1937). For the protection of the passengers and crew security installations and rescue facilities on board the Hapag-Lloyd ships have always been adapted to the newest technical standard, and on each voyage boat drill by the crew and instruction of the passengers about the security facilities are compulsory, so that everybody knows how to react in case of distress at sea.

THE COMMITTEE OF LLOYD'S
RECORD ON THIS TABLET
THE SERVICES RENDERED
BY THE CAPTAIN, OFFICERS AND CREW
OF THE STEAMER
"NEW YORK" (KOMMODORE FRITZ KRUSE)
ON THE OCCASION OF THE RESCUE
IN HEAVY WEATHER AND HIGH SEAS
OF THE CREW OF THE NORWEGIAN STEAMER
"SISTO"
WHICH WAS ABANDONED IN
LAT. 49. 8 N., LONG. 22. 18 W.,
ON THE 19TH DECEMBER, 1934.
LLOYD'S MEDALS FOR SAVING LIFE AT SEA
WERE AWARDED BY THE COMMITTEE
TO THOSE WHO MANNED THE BOAT
WHICH EFFECTED THE RESCUE.

Lloyds of London awarded the lifeboat crew of the Hapag-steamer "New York", who rescued the Norwegian crew of the "Sisto" in heavy weather, in a ceremony the rescue medal pictured opposite.

The merger (1970)

Once the decision had been taken by Hapag and Lloyd to containerise their liner trades as from 1968 onwards, it was a logical and consistent step for the two companies to merge their assets. The new investments amounting to more than one billion marks, that were required to set up container operations in three major trades in quick succession, namely, the North Atlantic, Australia and the Far East, by far exceeded any previous liner projects put together. More than ever economic pressure existed for rationalizing resources and for coordinating operations and schedules to achieve a better utilization of capacities, and, above all, to raise the necessary funds for this new and revolutionary transport system. After the war, all but three liner services had already been operated by both companies jointly with new and almost identical ship types.

Credit must, no doubt, be paid to the Executive Boards and their Chairmen Werner Traber (Hapag) and Richard Bertram (Lloyd) for not only having led, in close consultation with the major shareholders, the two shipping companies to the top rank of international shipping for a third time within 20 years, but also, with the right timing, to have taken the necessary steps towards a merger in order to provide a broader capital backing with a view to meeting the new requirements of the container age. They left their houses in good order to their successors, which now had to be furnished with foresight for the new tasks. A new generation of managers took over the command. It was free of resentment towards the traditional rivalries between the two homeports, that time and again had stood in the way of any "rapprochement". An agreement was soon reached on the financial evaluation of the companies' assets and on the organizational aspects, and, at extraordinary meetings of the two Supervisory Boards, it was unanimously agreed that the two companies would formally merge on August 31st, 1970, with retroactive effect as from January 1st, 1970. These decisions were confirmed at the two stockholders' general meetings in July 1970. The rate of conversion was fixed at 1:1 for Lloyd and 11:13 for Hapag stocks. It thus terminated the individual existence of the two great rivals, after 123 years of most dramatic development, which made them the two top commercial enterprises in their native cities.

Even then the interests of the two city-states, to whom these shipping lines were so closely attached, had to be balanced carefully and was reflected in the decision to maintain two parallel headquarters, a unique feature for German corporations. Most of the freight liner traffic departments were based in Hamburg, whilst the passenger and cruising department, together with the headquarters of the vast travel bureau organization, as well as the bulker and tanker fleet activities of the newly established "Kosmos" shipping company, were stationed, among others, in Bremen. The new house flag and funnel colours, too, symbolized the joint activities of its parent companies. While Lloyd's flag was adopted with its blue key and anchor crossed on a white background, the funnels of the cargo liners were painted in Hapag's impressive buff, with its black-white-red top.

At the end of 1970, the amalgamated fleet of Hapag-Lloyd comprised, according to its first Annual Report, 100 cargo ships and 6 cellular container ships, with a total capacity of more than one million tons deadweight, as well as two passenger ships, the "Bremen" and the "Europa", with a combined passenger capacity of nearly 2,000.

The companies had a joint workforce of 8,260 in the shipping and tourism sector, of which 6,580 were employed on board ships.

These ships moved 6.8 m freight tons in 1970, plus 37,300 passengers. The great structural changes, which have since taken place in liner shipping are perhaps best exemplified by comparative figures for 1990. At the end of that year the company employed 7,500 people in the shipping and tourism sector, of which just 900 worked on board ships. The number of liner vessels had dropped to 21, with a combined deadweight tonnage of 750,000. The volume transported, however, had increased by nearly 50 % to over 10 m freight tons p. a. The new "Europa" took 13,700 passengers to many exciting destinations.

1.9.1970: Merger of the two biggest German shipping companies forming Hapag-Lloyd AG, Hamburg/Bremen. North German Lloyd's flag becomes the new company flag, while the funnels of the cargo liners were painted in Hapag's impressive buff, with its black-white-red top.

1.1.1987: The corporate-wide activities especially in the tourist section, require a new uniform company emblem, which found its expression in a new house flag (picture) and in the colours cognac with a blue logo, which have already become a trade mark for the passengers of Hapag-Lloyd's charter airline and of the cruise ship "Europa" since the seventies.

Turbulent North Atlantic (1983–1993)

The high hopes of the North Atlantic carriers, that their tremendous capital investments in this new container-system would provide them with an adequate return on investment in the late sixties and seventies and thereby contribute to a much-needed stabilization of this important trade route, seemed to work out until the mid-seventies. Two adverse developments, however, a sharp decline in cargo volume in the wake of the two energy crises in 1975 and 1979 and an overproduction of ship capacities provoked by a world-wide subsidization of shipyards which induced increased speculative ordering – led to a total destabilization of the market and resulted in a tumbling of ocean freight rates. Thus the North Atlantic again became the dumping ground for a growing number of short-lived carriers, making it impossible for the established lines to earn a reasonable return on their longterm investments.

This is, however, only one side of the coin. The other is the competitive environment, created by the US shipping regulation. It was based on an outdated regime established in 1916, which in the past years had been misinterpreted and in its consequences eroded beyond recognition by a series of US court decisions taken due to a lack of knowledge of commercial necessities. This regulation has prevented conference carriers in the US trades from rationalizing and organising their international liner services to the extent necessary to reduce operational and handling costs to a minimum. Above all, it prohibited the possibility of offering the full benefits of containerization to the US trade achievable only through a concerted door-to-door service.

Between 1980 and 1983 carriers again engaged in an ocean rate war inflicting heavy losses for all participants, in the vague hope of redressing the market balance. Unstable trades and their inherent imponderables only result, however, in short-lived price advantages for shippers. Time and again the market has proved to be the strongest of all regulators, so long as it is not imbalanced by political, or governmental intervention, of which oversubsidization is the most ominous. Governments, from whatever direction, should therefore not unilaterally extend national law into international activities and try to compete with business "know-how". The reform of the US shipping regulation, which was passed by the US Congress in March 1984 after several years hard work and which took effect as the new Shipping Act in June 1984, tried to take account of modern transport requirements to a greater extent than hitherto. Whether the high hopes that have been attached to it can be fulfilled, will remain to be seen after its final passage through the American Congress in 1992/93 and in its practical application thereafter. Should it not be possible to curtail government or supra-governmental intervention in international ocean trades to a tolerable degree, it will with all likelihood lead to a further destabilization of US and adjacent ocean trades or, alternatively, result in state-licensed, bilateral traffic rights of an IATA type for shipping lines, with all the negative consequences for the trade.

The emergence of further container operators such as Evergreen, Maersk and Nedlloyd in the North Atlantic may cause a renewed erosion of ocean freight rates in the nineties as a consequence of underutilised overcapacities. This development prompted Hapag-Lloyd to join forces with another operator, the Atlantic Container Line (ACL), as of June 1986 by coordinating their schedules and through the conclusion of a slotcharter agreement as a further step towards rationalization. In order to harmonise the tonnage to be employed, Hapag-Lloyd had its 4 North Atlantic vessels jumboised from 1750 TEU to 2594 TEU in the second half of 1985 at the Blohm & Voss AG shipyard, Hamburg. The new joint service offers the trade the advantage that henceforth Gothenburg, and with it Scandinavia, will also be served directly on a weekly basis.

The gradual introduction of the container in international seaborne trade a quarter of a century ago triggered a transport revolution which meanwhile has extended to nearly all countries of the globe. It is no longer the ocean ship but the container that today stands in the centre of transport events. In trans-ocean door-to-door services the shipowner has developed from a mere ocean transport operator to a combined transport operator, the so-called CTO, who endeavours to offer his clients a comprehensive service package geared to their individual transport requirements. It commences with stowage consultancy for the shipper whilst the goods are still in the production process, extends to data support in the booking

The containership "Humboldt Express", 34,000 tdw, 2,081 TEU, 19 knots, is one of the youngest and most modern ships of the Hapag-Lloyd fleet. Early 1984 she embarked upon her maiden voyage in the new full container service of the Europe-South America Lines (EUROSAL) to the West Coast of South America. Also in this trade Hapag-Lloyd has as a German carrier offered a high quality dependable liner service for 118 years.

EUROSAL forms a further link in the world-wide Hapag-Lloyd container chain with the aim of offering multi-modal transports from country to country and from door to door.
These multi-purpose containerships cannot only transport containers, including reefer containers, but, tuned to the requirements of the trade, also break bulk or general cargo, as well as oversized pieces. A 30-t-gantry crane makes these ships to a large degree independent from shoreside discharging and loading facilities in the South American ports. Their main engines operate with heavy fuel in combination with a newly developed after ship, resulting in an extremely low daily fuel consumption.

A Hamburg streetcar destined for the "Steuben Parade" in New York is lifted on board on a container flat.

A 40'-Container on an American highway – in the background the snow-covered peak of Mount Hood in the Rocky Mountains: it is no longer the ship, but the whole door-to-door transport of containers that is offered to shippers in an intermodal service. The container's superior economics lie in its efficient stowage and careful handling, its simplified and speedy documentation and short transit times. These are the latest quality parameters of a combined transport operator, the CTO.

The Hamburg headoffice of the Hapag-Lloyd group at Ballindamm.

67

Atlantic-bridge
365 days a year

process, delivery of the suitable container equipment, simplified documentation and ends with the delivery of the container "just in time" at the receiver's premises.

Thus the shipowner becomes the most important partner of the shipper in his logistical distribution chain. With the background of such a variety of service aspects, the superficial discussion about the level of ocean freight rates takes on a totally different perspective. It is no longer the quality of the export good alone, but rather the close cooperation as partners between the shipping industry and the liner shipping companies in the logistical field which will help the client to remain competitive in future in the hotly contested international markets.

Hapag-Lloyd on course 2000: a further spectacular step into the future was brought about by the commissioning of the multi-purpose container ships "Bonn Express" and "Heidelberg Express" in March and May 1989 as prototypes of the ship 2000 that has been developed by Hapag-Lloyd for worldwide employment. With their highly modern technological equipment, these ships sail with an integrated crew of 12–14 men only and are connected via satellites with the worldwide communications network. All technical functions of the vessel's operation can be controlled by one officer from the bridge, which has now evolved into a Ship Operation Centre (SOC).

The Safety Centre is also located in the SOC — representing a further step towards enhancing safety by enabling the crew to take rapid action during emergencies.

Special attention has been dedicated in the vessel's design to environmental protection, by applying standards aboard the new ships which are well in advance of today's statutory requirements. All dry and wet waste is segregated and collected in the central refuse centre or in suitable tanks for later removal into the appropriate installations in port.

With this futuristic ship operation concept under German flag, all officers and crew members receive extensive academic and practical training which leads to professional competence for the entire ship operation and ensures an optimum working organisation. Their living quarters can be compared with that of a luxurious cruise vessel. The two ships are employed in the US-Gulf/South Atlantic service.

Coordination and cooperation — basic prerequisites for a stable bridge

Liner conferences have become the target for public criticism as allegedly antiquated anti-competitive cartels, which should be abolished as soon as possible, not only in the USA but also in Europe in the past couple of years. They are, however, similar to the form of democratic government, of which Winston Churchill once sarcastically remarked, that it has certainly many weaknesses, however, one should cling to it as long as nothing better has been found.

Liner conferences, a rough definition of which is given in the notes on page 81, came into being in the wake of the inauguration of the Suez Canal in 1869 when the shortened distances to the Eastern Hemisphere caused a tremendous oversupply of steamship tonnage and, as a consequence, a total collapse of freight rates.

It is the comprehensive term for a great variety of rate agreements and conditions between otherwise independent competitors in ocean liner shipping on certain routes which could also be called temporary peace treaties in an otherwise ruthless struggle for market shares.

The remarkable summary on liner shipping of the famous "Alexander Report" on "Steamship Agreements and Affiliations" by the Committee on the Merchant Marine and Fisheries of the US House of Representatives of 1914, named after its chairman Hon. Yoshua W. Alexander, which reflects the findings of a painstaking investigation of shipping combinations, is as true today as it was 75 years ago:

"The entire history of steamship agreements shows that in ocean commerce there is no happy medium between war and peace when several lines engage in the same trade. Most of the numerous agreements and conference arrangements discussed in the foregoing report were the outcome of rate wars, and represent a truce between the contending lines."

"To terminate existing agreements would necessarily bring about one of two results: the lines would either engage in rate wars which would mean the elimination of the weak and the survival of the strong, or, to avoid a costly struggle, they would consolidate through common ownership. Neither result can be prevented by legislation, and either would mean a monopoly fully as effective, and it is believed more so, than can exist by virtue of an agreement. Moreover, steamship agreements and conferences are not confined to the lines engaging in the foreign trade of the United States. They are as universally used in the foreign trade of other countries as in our own. The merchants of these countries now enjoy the foregoing advantages of cooperative arrangements, and to restore open and cutthroat competition among the lines serving the United States would place American exporters at a disadvantage in many markets as compared with their foreign competitors."

These facts are fundamentally the same today. The implementation and maintenance of dependable longterm high quality port-to-port and door-to-door liner and container services needs stability and a positive financial climate. Otherwise it will become an incalculable risk for any private carrier.

The US-Trans-Atlantic and Trans-Pacific trades have become the most destabilized liner trades in the world, with the highest rate of fluctuation and financial collapse.

Liner shipping and world trade must, through coordination and cooperation, find a basis for a sound business relationship if they are expected to work effectively on a long term basis, and if the cost of ocean and intermodal transport is to be kept at reasonable levels. In order to realize these principles, adequate political frameworks, which have to be synchronized to reflect the interests of all trading partners in order to avoid exterritorial conflicts, with the aim of promoting true competition and not furthering the subsidization race, are a fundamental necessity.

I have tried to highlight the ups and downs of 140 years of ocean transportation across the Atlantic, and perhaps you, the reader, will agree that it is a fascinating story. To keep the bridge across the Atlantic intact, remains a prime objective of Hapag-Lloyd: with the quality of service, which this company has continuously developed, ever since its first clipper made its maiden voyage to the New World in October of 1848.

Transport Facilities of the Hapag-Lloyd Group

(as of 31st of December 1990)

Liner Shipping

No.	Type	Name	Year Built/ Jumboised	Service Speed kn	TEU*	DWT
I.		**Container ships**				
1.	CMS	Pol Baltic (ex Leverkusen Express)	1970/78	20.5	1 060	21 307
2.	CMS	Pol Gulf (ex Ludwigshafen Express)	1970/79	20.5	1 060	21 185
3.	CTS	Canada Express	1970	21.5	1 685	34 883
4.	CTS	Bremen Express	1972/82	23.0	2 950	47 838
5.	CTS	Hongkong Express	1972/82	23.0	2 950	47 838
6.	CTS	Hamburg Express	1972/82	23.0	2 950	47 733
7.	CTS	Tokio Express	1973/81	23.0	2 950	47 733
8.	CMS	Windward	1974/79	16.0	978	21 885
9.	CMS	Woermann Ulanga (ex Caribia Express)	1976	20.0	1 386	23 047
10.	CMS	Sierra Express	1977	20.0	1 474	28 152
11.	CMS	Stuttgart Express	1977/85	20.5	2 594	40 624
12.	CMS	Düsseldorf Express	1977/85	20.5	2 594	40 624
13.	CMS	Nürnberg Atlantic (ex Nürnberg Express)	1978/85	20.5	2 594	40 624
14.	CMS	Köln Atlantic (ex Köln Express)	1978/85	20.5	2 594	40 624
15.	CMS	America Express	1978	20.0	1 582	28 152
16.	CMS	Alemania Express	1978	20.0	1 582	28 152
17.	CMS	Frankfurt Express	1981	23.0	3 430	51 540
18.	CMS	Humboldt Express	1984	18.5	2 181	34 037
19.	CMS	Bonn Express	1989	21.0	2 291	36 000
20.	CMS	Heidelberg Express	1989	21.0	2 291	36 000
21.	CMS	Berlin Express	1990	21.0	2 716	42 221
					45 892	760 199

CMS = Container motor ship   CTS = Container turbine ship
* Capacity in 20′ container units

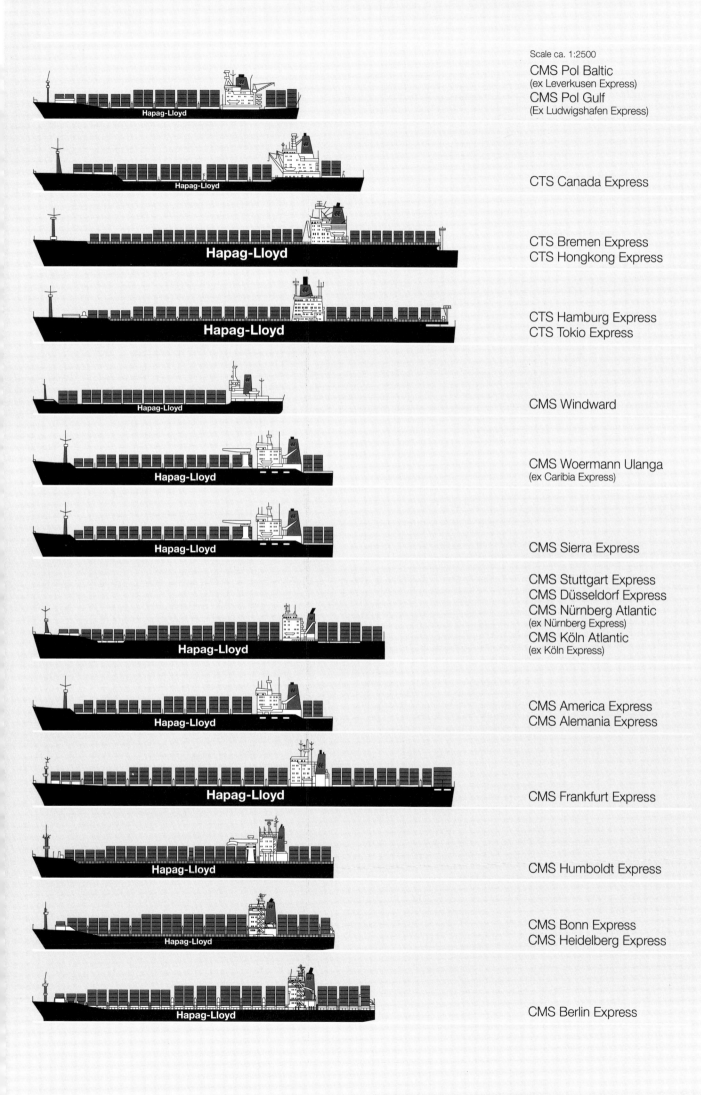

Scale ca. 1:2500

CMS Pol Baltic
(ex Leverkusen Express)
CMS Pol Gulf
(Ex Ludwigshafen Express)

CTS Canada Express

CTS Bremen Express
CTS Hongkong Express

CTS Hamburg Express
CTS Tokio Express

CMS Windward

CMS Woermann Ulanga
(ex Caribia Express)

CMS Sierra Express

CMS Stuttgart Express
CMS Düsseldorf Express
CMS Nürnberg Atlantic
(ex Nürnberg Express)
CMS Köln Atlantic
(ex Köln Express)

CMS America Express
CMS Alemania Express

CMS Frankfurt Express

CMS Humboldt Express

CMS Bonn Express
CMS Heidelberg Express

CMS Berlin Express

Liner Shipping

Container Type	Number 20' Containers	Number 40' Containers	Total Number
II. Containers*			
Standard Containers	35 340	24 560	59 900
High Cube Containers	–	2 280 **	2 280
Hardtop Containers	1 455	300	1 755
Open Top Containers	1 144	1 952	3 096
Flats	892	1 318	2 210
Platforms	96	74	170
Ventilated Containers	5 157	–	5 157
Insolated Containers	1 206	705	1 911
Refrigerated Containers	908	795	1 703
Refrigerated Containers (Diesel)	-	1 886	1 886
Bulk Containers	805	–	805
Tank Containers	451	–	451
Total Containers	47 454	33 870	81 324
Total TEU	47 454	67 740	115 200
III. Trailers*	1 768	4 079	5 847

* Hapag-Lloyd owned or longterm leased   ** 45'

Standard Containers
Suitable for every normal cargo.
20' and 40'

Ventilated Containers
Specifically for cargoes requiring
ventilation. 20'

High Cube Containers
Specifically for light, voluminous cargoes
or those for excessive height. 40'

Insulated Containers
Specifically for cargoes requiring transport at a constant temperature above or
below freezing point. This is controlled by
the ship's or terminal's cooling plant or a
clip-on reefer unit. 20' and 40'

Hardtop Containers
With removable solid steel roof.
Specifically for heavy lifts, cargoes of
excessive height, for loading from
above (e.g. by crane), loading from door
end with removable door header.
20' and 40'

Reefer Containers
Specifically for cargoes requiring transport at a constant temperature above or
below freezing point. With built-in reefer
unit. 20' and 40'

Open Top Containers
With removable tarpaulin. Specifically for
cargoes of excessive height, for loading
from above (e.g. by crane), loading from
door end with removable door header.
20' and 40'

Bulk Containers
Specifically for loose/bulk cargoes,
e.g. malt. 20'

Flats
Specifically for heavy-lifts and overwidth
cargoes. Non-containerizable cargo can
be accommodated on several flats
positioned side by side. 20' and 40'

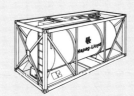

Tank Containers
Specifically for liquid chemicals. A limited
number of containers are deployed
exclusively for the transport of liquors
and liquid foods. 20'

Platforms
Specifically for heavy-lifts and out of
gauge cargoes. Non-containerizable
cargo can be accommodated on several
platforms lashed together (not for Inland
Transport). 20' and 40'

Tourism

	No.	Type	Seats	Call Sign	Commis-sioning
I. Airplanes					
	1.	Boeing 727/100	130	D-AHLM	1973/1984
	2.	Boeing 727/100	130	D-AHLS	1976/1987
	3.	Airbus A 310/200	264	D-AHLW	1988
	4.	Airbus A 310/200	264	D-AHLV	1988
	5.	Airbus A 310/200	264	D-AHLZ	1988
	6.	Airbus A 310/200	264	D-AHLX	1988
	7.	Airbus A 310/300	237	D-AHLA	1989
	8.	Airbus A 310/300	237	D-AHLB	1990
	9.	Boeing 737/400	167	D-AHLJ	1989
	10.	Boeing 737/400	167	D-AHLK	1989
	11.	Boeing 737/400	167	D-AHLL	1989
	12.	Boeing 737/400	167	D-AHLO	1989
	13.	Boeing 737/400	167	D-AHLP	1989
	14.	Boeing 737/400	167	D-AHLQ	1990
	15.	Boeing 737/400	167	D-AHLR	1990
	16.	Boeing 737/500	128	D-AHLE	1990
	17.	Boeing 737/500	128	D-AHLD	1990
	18.	Boeing 737/500	128	D-AHLF	1990

	Built in	GT	Service Speed kn
II. Passenger ship			
ms **Europa**	1981	37 012	21,0

Scale ca. 1:500

Boeing 727/100

Airbus A 310/200

Airbus A 310/300

Boeing 737/400

Boeing 737/500

Scale ca. 1:1500

ms **Europa**

Port and
Coastal Services

No.	Name	Built in	HP	DWT
I.	**Tugs***			
1.	Castor	1963	1 350	
2.	Pollux	1963	1 350	
3.	Comet	1967	1 600	
4.	Stella	1967	1 320	
5.	Triton	1967	1 320	
6.	Vesta	1967	1 320	
7.	Cyclop	1968	1 600	
8.	Wega	1968	1 320	
9.	Accurat	1968	1 320	
10.	Escort	1970	600	
11.	Mercur	1972	2 000	
12.	Planet	1973	2 000	
13.	Saturn	1973	2 000	
14.	Rasant	1973	2 000	
15.	Resolut	1974	2 000	
16.	Herkules	1977	2 640	
17.	Sirius	1977	2 520	
18.	Steinbock	1977	2 520	
19.	Arion	1978	2 970	
20.	Bär	1982	2 200	
21.	Mars	1982	2 200	
22.	Parat	1983	2 400	
23.	Constant	1987	2 502	
24.	Stier	1990	2 502	
II.	**Anchor handling tug supply vessels***			
1.	Safe	1983	9 280	1 900
2.	Sound	1983	9 280	1 900
III.	**Additional Transportation Forms** (without propulsion)*			
1.	River craft L 1 (special barge)	1974		2 350
2.	Transport ponton P 5	1974		4 800
3.	Transport ponton P 7	1976		9 500
4.	Flat top barge P 10	1978		25 000

* Watercraft owned by Hapag-Lloyd Transport & Service GmbH and Lütgens & Reimers GmbH

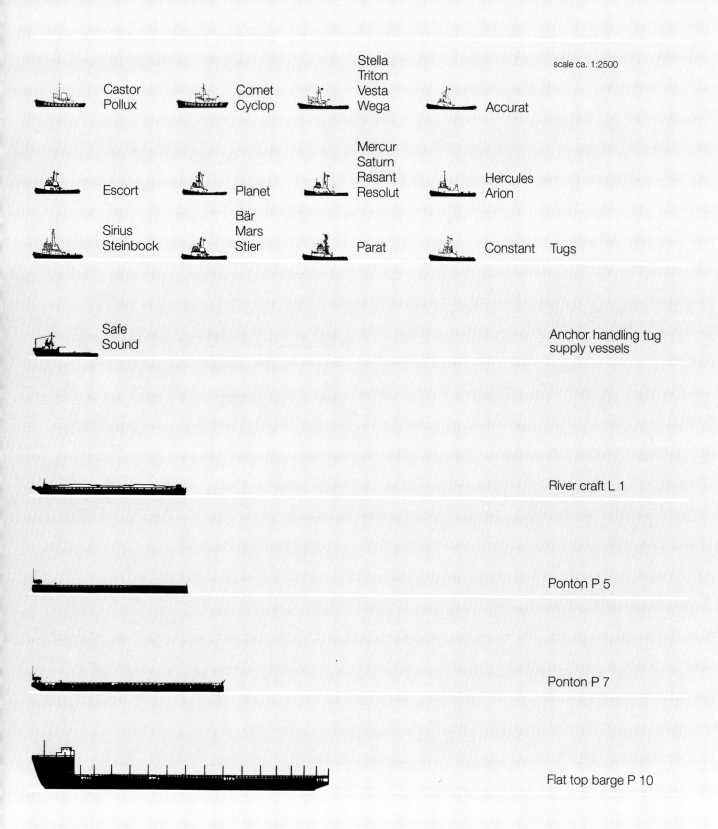

scale ca. 1:2500

Castor
Pollux

Comet
Cyclop

Stella
Triton
Vesta
Wega

Accurat

Escort

Planet

Mercur
Saturn
Rasant
Resolut

Hercules
Arion

Sirius
Steinbock

Bär
Mars
Stier

Parat

Constant   Tugs

Safe
Sound

Anchor handling tug
supply vessels

River craft L 1

Ponton P 5

Ponton P 7

Flat top barge P 10

The Hapag-Lloyd Group at a glance

Liner shipping:
Liner services connect Europe with all
parts of the world except Africa

21 container ships totalling 45,900 TEU

Employees 1990: 3,769
Revenues 1990: DM 2,075 m

Port and coastal services:
Employees 1990: 461
Revenues 1990: DM 90 m

24 Tugs

2 Offshore supply vessels
Management of Antarctic research
vessel Polarstern

Forwarding:
Employees 1990: 755
Revenues 1990: DM 235 m

Tourism:
Employees 1990: 3,143
Revenues 1990: DM 1,100 m
Air charter
6 A 310 – 10 Boeing 737 – 2 Boeing 727

Worldwide cruising
with ms **Europa**

Travel agency network
with over 100 offices

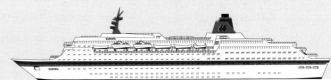

The Hapag-Lloyd Group
Employees 1990: 8,128
Revenues 1990: DM 3,500 m

Acknowledgement and bibliography

This book is the second revised and updated edition of a private publication brought out by Hapag-Lloyd AG in 1983 under the title "Bridge across the Atlantic". It has been based on a number of earlier publications by Hapag-Lloyd AG and its founder companies Hamburg-America Line, Hamburg and North German Lloyd, Bremen, of the files from the company archives in Hamburg and Bremen, as well as on the writer's own research. The comments and conclusions drawn are the sole responsibility of the author.

The author would like to thank a number of people who contributed materially to the production of the manuscript. This refers in particular to Miss Andrea Emily Stumpf, then graduate student in International Studies at the University of North Carolina and Chapel Hill, N. C., who spent her summer internship as a Morehead Scholar partly in his Department in 1983, and was a great help in doing part of the research and by streamlining the texts to a more readable English. From the company's staff Mr. H. Rickmann, former Head of the Publicity Department, not only greatly encouraged but also shaped and coordinated the design of the first edition. Hapag-Lloyd's two archivists, Mrs. Erika Lisson, Bremen, and Mr. Rolf Finck, Hamburg, compiled all the original documents, ads, posters and pictures that helped to revive the historical events. Mr. Dirk Möller was responsible for the arrangement and proper balancing between text and illustrations. Mr. Douglas Ahrens and Mr. Peter Hall, despite heavy work pressures, read and amended the English proved copies of the first and second edition. Mrs. Kerstin Giessen and Mrs. Andrea Neumann typed the manuscripts while Mrs. Regina Meinecke is responsible for the production of the fine book cover. I would thank in particular the publisher Gerhard Bollmann and his production manager Heinz Kameier for the total reprint in its new edition.

This book is based among others on the following sources:

Annual reports of the Hamburg-America Line, North German Lloyd and Hapag-Lloyd AG from 1847–1989. Hapag-Lloyd archive, Hamburg (files, contracts, protocols, memoirs, manuscripts).

Baasch, E.: Beiträge zur Geschichte der Handelsbeziehungen zwischen Hamburg und Amerika. Hamburg 1892.

Behrens, C.B.A.: Merchant Shipping and the Demands of War. London 1955.

Bessell, Georg: Norddeutscher Lloyd 1857–1957. Bremen 1957.

Bonsor, N.R.P.: North Atlantic Seaway. Prescot, Lancash. 1955.

Bromme, Traugott: Rathgeber für Auswanderungslustige. 1846.

Cecil, Lamar: Albert Ballin – Business and Politics in Imperial Germany 1888–1918, Princeton, 1967.

Corbett, Sir Julian S.: Naval Operations. London 1920.

Fayle, Ernest C.: Seaborne Trade. London 1920.

Geissler, Robert: Hamburg. Ein Führer durch die Stadt und ihre Umgebung. Leipzig 1861.

Gelberg, Birgit: Auswanderung nach Übersee. Soziale Probleme der Auswandererbeförderung in Hamburg und Bremen von der Mitte des 19. Jahrhunderts bis zum Ersten Weltkrieg. Hamburg 1973.

Hamburg und seine Bauten unter Berücksichtigung der Nachbarstädte Altona und Wandsbek 1914. Hg. v. Architekten- und Ingenieurs-Verein zu Hamburg; 2 Bde. Hamburg 1914.

Helfferich, Emil: Ein Leben, Bd. 4, Privatdruck 1964.

Himer, Kurt: 75 Jahre Hamburg-Amerika-Linie; 2 Bde. Hamburg 1922.

House of Representatives: Proceedings of the Committee of the Merchant Marine and Fisheries in the "Investigation of Shipping Combinations" under House Resolution 587, 62/63rd Congress, Washington 1914, Vol. 4.

Huckriede-Schulz, L.: Die Deutsche Schiffahrt und ihre Männer. Hamburg 1929.

Huldermann, Bernhard: Albert Ballin, 6. Aufl. Oldenburg 1922.

Kludas, Arnold, und Bischoff, Herbert: Die Schiffe der Hamburg-Amerika-Linie 1847–1970; 3 Bde. Herford 1980.

Kludas, Arnold: Die Geschichte der deutschen Passagierschiffahrt 1850–1990, 5 vols., Hamburg 1986/90.

Kohlhaus, Heinz-Hellmut: Die Hapag, Cuno und das Deutsche Reich, 1920–1933. Hamburg 1952.

Landerer, R.: Geschichte der Hamburg-Amerikanischen Packetfahrt-Actiengesellschaft, Hamburg 1897.

Mathies, Otto: Hamburgs Reederei 1814–1914. Hamburg 1924.

Mönckmeier, Wilhelm: Die deutsche überseeische Auswanderung. Jena 1921.

Moltmann, Günter (Hg.): Deutsche Amerikaauswanderung im 19. Jahrhundert. Sozialgeschichtliche Beiträge. (Amerikastudien, Bd. 44). Stuttgart 1976.

Murken, Erich: Die großen transatlantischen Linienreederei-Verbände, Pools und Interessengemeinschaften bis zum Ausbruch des Weltkrieges. Jena 1922.

Museum für Hamburgische Geschichte: ". . . nach Amerika". Auswanderung in die Vereinigten Staaten. 200 Jahre Vereinigte Staaten von Amerika 1976.

Neubaur, Paul: Der Norddeutsche Lloyd – 50 Jahre der Entwicklung, 1857–1907; 2 Bde. Leipzig 1907.

Petzet, Arnold: Heinrich Wiegand – ein Lebensbild. Bremen 1932.

Philippovich, Eugen von (Hg.): Auswanderung und Auswanderungspolitik in Deutschland. Berichte über die Entwicklung und den gegenwärtigen Zustand des Auswanderungswesens in den Einzelstaaten und im Reich. (Schriften des Vereins für Socialpolitik 52). Leipzig 1892.

Schinckel, Max von: Lebenserinnerungen. Hamburg 1928.

Steinweg, Günther: Die Deutsche Handelsflotte im Zweiten Weltkrieg. Göttingen 1954.

Sthamer: Die Auswanderungshallen in Hamburg. Hg. v. der Hamburg-Amerika-Linie. Hamburg 1900.

Stödter, Rolf: Schicksalsjahre deutscher Seeschiffahrt 1945–1955. Herford 1982.

Wätjen, Hermann: Aus der Frühzeit des Nordatlantikverkehrs. Leipzig 1932.

Webster, Donald Dent: Harmful and unintended Effects of the Shipping Act of 1916, as amended, interpreted and administered since 1961. Washington D.C. 1970.

Witthöft, Hans-Jürgen: Hapag – Hamburg-Amerika Linie. Herford 1973.

Witthöft, Hans-Jürgen: Norddeutscher Lloyd. Herford 1973.

Explanatory Notes for Abbreviations

ton(s) = grt = gross register ton is the cubic capacity of the permanently enclosed space of the ship (i.e. hull, superstructure, deckhouses etc.) calculated on the basis of 100 cubic feet being equal to one gross ton. Source: Lloyd's Register.

dwt = tons deadweight = carrying capacity of a ship in metric tons including bunkers and stores.

knots = nautical miles per hour, indicating service speed. 1 knot = 1.850 km p.h.

TEU = twenty foot equivalent unit = standard size for ocean containers, a forty foot container = 2 TEU.

CIP-Titelaufnahme
der Deutschen Bibliothek

Bridge across the Atlantic: The Story of Hapag Lloyd's North American Liner Services / Otto J. Seiler. –
Herford: Mittler, 1991
ISBN 3-8132-0365-4
NE: Seiler, Otto

Index

Definitions:

Shipping or liner conferences exist since 1875 and are "a group of two or more vessel-operating carriers which provides international liner services for the carriage of passengers and/or cargo on a particular route or routes within specified geographical limits and which has an agreement or arrangement, whatever its nature, within the framework of which they operate under uniform or common passenger and/or freight rates and any other agreed conditions with respect to the provision of liner services."[1]

Today about 300 such conferences or rate agreements exist worldwide. Large shipping companies are usually members of several conferences depending on the number of routes they serve.

[1] as defined by the UNCTAD Convention on a Code of Conduct for Liner Conferences; for the sake of completeness the words "passengers and/or" have been added by the author.

Ships

Central point of the new concept:
The bridge as Ship Operation Centre with panoramic visibility. Captain Dieter Zapff in the star-board shifted cockpit. The entire ship operation is controlled from the bridge by one ship operation officer. The engine-room control centre has been made redundant.

Ship 2000:
A new concept is launched.

The container ships "Bonn Express" and "Heidelberg Express", which were commissioned in 1989, are the prototypes of the "ship 2000" of Hapag-Lloyd, whose technical design introduces a new revolutionary age in ship operation. By their high degree of automatisation these ships are manned by a crew of only 14, who receive special training for that purpose. A generous layout of rooms provides the necessary comfort for the crew including leisure time facilities as a compensation for their strenuous work.
The technical data:
container capacity 2,291 TEU, carrying capacity at a draft of 41 ft. about 34,800 t, length over all 677 ft., breadth 106 ft., service speed 21 knots.

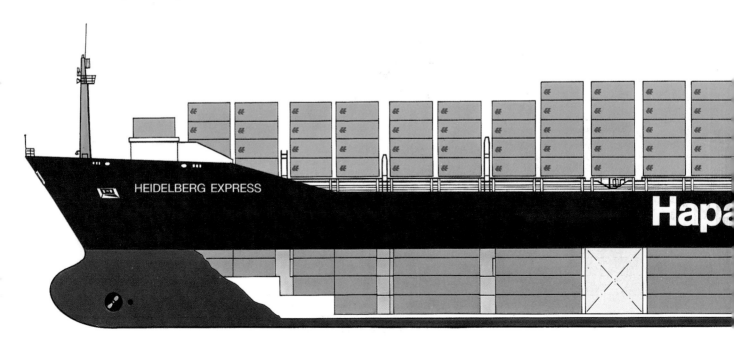